A CAR HAD SLOWED BEHIND HER . . .

Only when it had stopped and two men had leapt toward her from the car did it occur to her that she was their objective—and then only because a sudden blow to her jaw caused her to scream once, then have the scream choked off by a hand clapped over her mouth. From that moment on it was violence, helplessly yielded to, her mind aware only of pain and motion . . .

Such was the later graphic account of the troubled young wife who had left the Ala Wai Inn to escape a boresome party.

THE MASSIE CASE
The True Story

THE
MASSIE
CASE

by
Peter Packer
and
Bob Thomas

BANTAM BOOKS

TORONTO • NEW YORK • LONDON • SYDNEY • AUCKLAND

THE MASSIE CASE
A Bantam Book / December 1966
2nd printing . . . September 1984

Library of Congress Catalog Card Number: 66-29388

ISBN 0-553-24367-5

Published simultaneously in the United States and Canada

Bantam Books are published by Bantam Books, Inc. Its trade-
mark, consisting of the words "Bantam Books" and the por-
trayal of a rooster, is Registered in U.S. Patent and Trademark
Office and in other countries. Marca Registrada. Bantam
Books, Inc., 666 Fifth Avenue, New York, New York 10103.

PRINTED IN THE UNITED STATES OF AMERICA

H   11 10 9 8 7 6 5 4 3 2

ONE

Had Thalia Fortescue Massie been asked hypothetically, during the late summer of 1931, what her response might be to a report that her husband had killed a man to avenge her honor, her reply would have been direct and crushing. Tommy was hardly the type, she would have said, and really now, wasn't that sort of question awfully passé? It belonged in a stuffy, repression-choked Victorian parlor. Besides, she was quite capable of taking care of her "honor" by herself. Caustically, she might have added that if the question was intended as a devious route to her bedroom, her questioner was on the wrong track.

If there was perplexity, a questioning of her own identity and behavior, behind this forthright and sometimes cynical front which Thalia Massie presented to the world, it was seldom seen. Yet there must have been a need in her for self-understanding, since earlier that year, she had attempted a course in psychology at the University of Hawaii, a course which later, when she was on the witness stand, in her husband's defense, was to produce an outburst of which few had believed her capable.

In that year of 1931, Thalia was twenty years of age. It always surprised people to learn that she had been married for four years, for there was still about her some of the awkward and tentative qualities that go with adolescence. The languid mask of knowingness that she wore was a little forced. Behind the remote, impersonal stare in her unusually wide-set blue eyes, it seemed as though there were a wary seeking for the tender, personal bond which she would never admit she lacked, or needed. In the soft, round contours of her face there remained a childlike impermanence. She had still not overcome a tendency to let her shoulders droop, as though the burden of growing up were too much for her. Maturity, it seemed, had not caught up with her four years of marriage, though her tongue in its capacity for the acerbic thrust, the sarcastic parry, was that of a woman disenchanted, and much older. Her air of weary sophistication only partially concealed her youthful uncertainties.

Thalia was the oldest of three daughters born to Mr. and Mrs. Granville Fortescue, both members of socially prominent families. Her father, Granville Roland Fortescue, author, war-correspondent, soldier, was a stepson of Robert R. Roosevelt, one-time United States Minister to the Netherlands and cousin to Theodore Roosevelt. Fortescue had seen action with the latter at the Battle of San Juan Hill. Later he became his military aide at the White House and was reported to have been adopted as a cousin by the President. Her mother, Grace Hubbard Bell Fortescue, was the daughter of Charles J. Bell, President of the American Security and Trust Company. It was a matter of pride with Mrs. Fortescue that she was related to the inventor of the telephone, Alexander Graham Bell. The activities of the Fortescues in those years, the social functions at which they were present, the births of their daughters, their foreign travels, were always to be found in the society pages of the Washington press.

Thalia's childhood, when she was not away at school, was spent on her maternal grandfather's estate near Washington, or at her parents' summer home (actually the home of her paternal grandfather, Robert R. Roosevelt) on a handsome, parklike property in Bayport, one of Long Island's privileged South Shore communities. In her early school years she attended the private Hillside School in Norwalk, Connecticut, transferring subsequently to the National Cathedral School for Girls in Washington.

The homes in which Thalia grew up were never quite her own, although she lost very little time making them so, especially the one at Bayport. The summers she spent there were a joyous and liberating time for her, a time of experimentation which grew more madcap and more daring as she grew older. Supervision was at a minimum, for her parents were away a great deal of the time, and neither gardener, caretaker nor the Filipino domestic help ever interfered.

There was the big house, the lake, the woods, the wide and private parkland. There were ponies to ride—bareback and naked if one felt like it. There were many times when Thalia did feel like it, unabashed by the stares of the section hands on the railroad beyond the estate.

A local resident who had known Thalia and her sisters all their lives, has recalled that "the girls were never given any home training whatever. They were allowed to run wild and do practically as they pleased at all times. During the summer months they practically lived in their bathing suits and went all over town in that manner.

"They had an old Ford," she remembered, "and an old Dodge car which they painted up in various gaudy colors and drove recklessly about the roads, attired only in their bathing costumes, with their feet and legs hanging out of the car."

That Thalia was not old enough to drive, did not seem to be a matter of concern to the local police.

"The girls did not associate with any of the young men or boys who were natives of this section," this observer added, "but did have young men friends who were from families of their own set, who came to this section for the summer or on visits. With these young men they would bathe in the lake at all hours of the night, very frequently as late as midnight."

Shocking though such behavior may have seemed to this neighbor, for Thalia it was both casual and exhilarating. The night swimming was best of all, for then one could peel to the skin more freely, plunge and play tag with "young men friends who were from families of their own set," then run back to the house to discover what new and exciting liquors were in the cabinet with which to warm shivering bodies and see how much they could hold without getting stoned, which adults, for some pathetic reason, invariably did, as they told themselves with patronizing sympathy.

It was all free play, self-indulgence, merry pranks for

Thalia during those glorious, hot Long Island summers. Especially the pranks. And why not? Hadn't her mother and her friends, to give one example, joined hands and roller-skated down Pennsylvania Avenue, refusing to halt until they had tied the traffic up in knots? Her mother's pranks may have been a youthful demonstration in behalf of a popular cause of that time, woman suffrage, but Thalia's pranks had no such idealistic purpose. They were her own impulsive outlet for high spirits, indulged in with all the zest and assurance to which she believed her seignioral rank entitled her, as was the prank she played during the summer of 1927, when she was sixteen.

There was a difference of opinion on whether or not it was a prank; certainly it was something much more alarming to the young mother who had left her baby asleep in its carriage in the lobby of a Patchogue, Long Island, theater that evening. For the baby was gone when she came out of the theater, and Thalia was seen strolling away from the theater with the child in her arms.

Thalia was arrested. The original charge was amended to one of disorderly conduct, and the case was dismissed. Thalia had managed to persuade the Judge that she had taken the baby from its carriage just for fun. Not that he, or the child's parents, or the local press, which reported the incident, saw it that way. She had merely meant it to be in the tradition of her mother's merry pranks she insisted. But there was only one person who seemed to understand— a young naval ensign who had been her partner in the prank, and who had been charged with her. She was very grateful to the ensign for understanding, and for bearing a good deal of the blame. Neither of them apparently saw anything particularly heinous about the incident, or believed that there was anything callous in their disregard for the feelings of a parent.

Thomas Hedges Massie, a graduate of Annapolis, had been commissioned an ensign in June of that year. He had been spending part of his leave before assignment in visiting friends on the island. Thalia was one of the girls to whom he had been introduced. Annapolis discipline could be readily shucked off in the company of a girl who knew no discipline, who kept open house for her friends and who could pour a drink of bourbon with all the charm and liberality of a hostess in his own native Kentucky. At twenty-two Ensign Massie was still young enough to feel flattered when he was told that he looked like Lindbergh in that year of Lindbergh adoration. It was not entirely untrue. There was indeed something of the young Lindbergh look about him, the small, well-shaped head, the boyish grin, the half-reticent, half-easy informality, the trim, slender figure. The crisp, white, brand-new ensign's uniform which he wore did nothing to hurt that image.

The incident at Patchogue brought Thalia and Tommy much closer together, although it was not necessarily the factor that brought them to their marriage, which took place on Thanksgiving Day of that year in the Bethlehem Chapel of the Washington Cathedral. If there were factors other than love which might have spurred the marriage, they were forgotten in the formal celebration of the wedding itself, sumptuously planned, traditionally solemnized. Fellow ensigns in full dress uniform formed a guard of honor for the married couple. At the reception which followed, Thalia flung her bouquet to her bridesmaids. The wedding had all the ingredients of a fairy tale in which prince and princess lived happily ever after, although it was reported that when Robert R. Roosevelt heard of the marriage upon his return from abroad he said that had he been in the country he would not have permitted Massie to be forced into a marriage of that sort.

It was apparently a restless and discontented wife rather than a blissful princess who accompanied her husband when he was assigned to Pearl Harbor in 1930 after a tour of duty on the mainland. It did not take Thalia long to discover that for the wife of a junior officer in the peacetime Navy stationed at Pearl Harbor, life could be deadly in its monotony. Naval personnel lived a life apart from the Islands—a closed society superimposed upon the native population and having very little to do either with its people or its government save in those areas which were in the Navy's logistical or defensive interest.

Although it is a part of the city, the district of Manoa Valley, where Thalia and Tommy lived, looks down on Honolulu from its verdant eminence with Olympian detachment.

Its streets climb the hill on a steep gradient, thrusting a broad swath of sunlit upland plain into the dense, tropical depths of Oahu's rain forest reserve. Above the Manoa Valley, and to either side, lie the fluted, brooding green slopes of the Koolau Range which divides the lee from the windward side of the island. Spectacular rainbows are a gay, integral part of this profligate landscape. So are the countless waterfalls which plunge in a thin sparkle down the cool, furrowed heights of Mount Tantalus and the wind-buffeted escarpments of historic Nuuanu Pali.

It is of course no accident that the more prosperous Haoles—the white residents of Honolulu—made silk-stocking Manoa, as it is called, their preserve. So did many of the peacetime Army and Navy officers stationed in Honolulu during the early thirties. Its picturesque setting, its proximity to private schools, particularly to the renowned and exclusive Punahou School, which their children could attend without risk of contamination by alien cultures, the imaginative master plan of its secluded garden homes, the intricate network of its pleasant, shaded streets—all were calculated to form a reassuring barrier against the intrusion of the multi-ethnic city below.

Yet Honolulu was exile for Thalia, for once she had seen the Island sights, toured the sugar and pineapple fields, visited the historic shrines and landmarks of Hawaii's past, she was then compelled to fall back on her own resources. A year in the Islands taught her that her resources were very meager. It also taught her that neither a Lieutenant J.G. (the rank which Tommy now held), nor his wife, have very much social standing in the naval pecking order. It hadn't mattered so much on the mainland where there was opportunity to visit Long Island or Washington or New York. But here there was no escape. Lovely though it was, Manoa Valley was hardly Long Island's south shore. The enchanted little dream house on Kahawai Street where she and Tommy lived was hardly as big as the gardener's cottage at Bayport. The grounds, when compared with Bayside's parkland, were virtually nonexistent. Her world was confined to the home or to the homes of Navy wives like herself, to listening to their trivial bits of Navy gossip and scandal, to attending or hostessing the luncheons which they gave each other, to the Saturday night parties at which drinking was not a social lubricant but a determined ritual for achieving alcoholic stupor, the quicker the better.

Thalia drank too, and the more she drank the more sardonically candid she became in telling her husband's fellow officers how empty and futile were their lives, projecting her own discontent onto those around her. After a while, a good many of Tommy's friends did not care to have Thalia as a guest at their parties.

There was one Saturday evening in mid-September of 1931 when Tommy, returning home from duty at the Pearl Harbor submarine base, mentioned a party that was planned for that night.

To her, as she thought of it, the party was going to be another of those dreary, drunken brawls—another night of senseless whoopee (the word was in high favor then), with its inevitable Sunday hang-over.

She had spent the day in idleness, wearing a bathrobe, drifting from bedroom, to living room, kitchen—avoiding mirrors because they always gave back reflections she preferred not to see. She had made abortive attempts at conversation with Beatrice Nakamura, the Japanese maid. The petite, scrupulously clean and industrious domestic never really said anything except to murmur a few polite and unrevealing words in answer to a question. She seemed so self-sufficient, energetic, uncomplaining. It was remarkable that she could find so much to keep her busy when Thalia herself seemed unaware of anything that needed to be done. She would return Thalia's looks with a shy, enigmatic yet respectful smile, her subservience never changing no matter what she saw or heard.

Had she heard the breakfast squabbles, Thalia wondered, the bitter accusations and reproaches, the revelations of marital disenchantment?

Down there on the ewa (roughly western) side of the city, or wherever it was she lived among her own, Thalia may have reflected, they probably laughed themselves silly over the antics of Haole officers and their wives. Among her own . . . which she, Thalia Fortescue Massie, was not.

In this mood of self-searching misery, she told Tommy that she did not care to go, when he spoke of the party.

But he kept insisting. He and a couple of fellow officers had reserved a table at the Ala Wai Inn in Waikiki. He didn't intend to be put off by her apathy on the one night in the week when he could again shuck off Navy discipline and duty. And after some of the wrangling which had by now become an almost daily occurrence in their lives, Thalia agreed to go, perhaps because she did not want anyone to talk. She knew how Tommy hated people to suspect that their marriage was not all that it should be.

She joined him in a drink before going to dress, sure that this was going to be just another Saturday night brawl —and certainly without any premonition of the fact that a few hours hence the terrifying attack to which she would be subjected would set forces in motion that would come dangerously close to changing the course of Hawaii's history.

Of course the party was just as witless and depressing as she had known it would be . . . the dismal mockery of Island charm in the fake bamboo and hibiscus décor of the Ala Wai Inn . . . the melancholy Hawaiian music played by a native dance band (occasionally a request for an American number would break the honeyed, wailing pattern, but it sounded no different really), the hot press of bodies on the floor or in the airless *lanai* . . . the non-stop drinking of bootleg liquor in the booths.

The Ala Wai Inn on Kalakaua Avenue at the *ewa* approach to Waikiki was recognized as naval officers' territory on Saturday night. The few civilians who ventured in rarely stayed. Enlisted men stayed not at all. The noise, the crowd, the heat, the drunken laughter, the tropical artifice . . . the endless swapping of partners on the floor as soon as interest lagged or another man's partner seemed more desirable (all accepted with good grace among brother officers in whom jealousy had no place) . . . Thalia found it all growing more and more intolerable. Later, when she was questioned about that night, she said in terse understatement, "I was bored and tired of the party."

Tommy had left her alone in the booth while he went to dance with someone else. The two other officers in their group, with their wives, were off dancing or making the rounds of the booths. Thalia left her drink unfinished and wandered off to the private dining rooms on the upper floor. She was wearing a rather attractive long green beaded gown, cowled low at the bosom, its short sleeves trimmed with fur. A necklace of green beads hung about her neck. The color went well with her light coloring—the blonde shine of her long hair, which she wore coiled up and kept in place with a barrette.

If there was someone she expected to find in one of the private dining rooms, he was apparently not there, and her disappointment coupled with the chafing frustration which she felt—the feeling of being both "bored and tired of the party"—caused her to make a rather insulting remark to an officer who was dining with his wife and two other couples in another of the private dining rooms. They had ignored her—going on with their meal when she entered the room—and at once she was reproaching one of them for not being gentleman enough to rise and offer her a chair.

One could almost predict the exchanges that followed.

"I don't recall inviting you to join us," Thalia was told.

"And it's only by courtesy of the Navy that you're a gentleman!" was Thalia's retort.

"Thalia," she was coolly informed then, "I think you're a louse!"

There were ramifications to the term which cast aspersions on her behavior much deeper than the squabble of the moment and which Thalia had no intention of letting pass. She at once and with some force slapped her opponent across the face.

In the uproar that followed, someone appealed "Get Tommy!" and while the women tried to calm Thalia before she thought of using her nails on him, and the men restrained their fellow officer, a waiter went to look for Tommy. But by that time, Thalia had had enough of it, turned from the room—and left the Inn.

Sometime around midnight—she was never exactly sure of the time when asked about it later—Thalia found herself on the John Ena Road, a narrow, curving but fairly well lighted thoroughfare which then connected Kalakaua Avenue with the Ala Moana—a broad boulevard which runs parallel to the sea, bordering the mauka (toward the mountains) limit of the Ala Moana Park and its beach. It is a street of small shops and cheap cafés such as are often found outside the gates of a military reservation. Fort de Russy, the Army post which sprawls down toward the beach from Kalakaua Avenue, lay barely a stone's throw from the John Ena Road, and the Ala Wai Inn. Like the shops which catered to the enlisted men of Fort de Russy, a cluster of wooden shacks crowded an alley just beyond the fort. These catered to a different hunger, drawing to the neighboring streets the strolling camp-followers to appease it.

Thalia intended, she was to say afterwards, "to walk a way on the road, then turn and walk back to the Ala Wai Inn." What her thoughts were in the course of that walk can only be guessed at. Had she, by striking a fellow officer, made life impossible for Tommy in Honolulu? She had been called a louse, virtually charged with behavior that in Tommy's code was unacceptable. Thoughts such as these may well have gone through her mind. At all events, she was much too preoccupied with her thoughts—smarting, resentful, homesick perhaps—to recall much of what she saw. She was not aware that a public dance was in progress at the now defunct Waikiki Park Pavilion, one of the entrances to which was on the John Ena Road. Nor was she aware of the saimin wagon at which customers stood drinking Japanese noodle soup, nor of the beauty parlor or the barber shop in both of which customers were still receiving attention.

A mile or two beyond where she walked, beyond the beach at Waikiki where only a handful of the luxury hotels now crowding the shore then existed, Diamond Head dipped its leonine shoulder into the sea, faintly silhouetted against the scented, luminous night sky. Of this, too, she was all but oblivious. She walked, as she subsequently recalled, "with my head down." It was characteristic of her to walk that way, her shoulders drooping, indulging the introspection, the need for self-understanding, which baffled her.

Thus, so unaware of all but herself—certainly not imagining that a woman walking alone at such an hour might be taken for a streetwalker in that area—she paid no attention to the fact that a car had slowed behind her close to the curb, that it seemed to be keeping pace with her. Only when it had stopped and two men had leapt toward her from the car did it occur to her that she was their objective—and then only because a sudden blow to her jaw caused her to scream once, then have the scream choked off by a hand clapped over her mouth. From that moment on it was violence, helplessly yielded to, her mind aware only of pain and motion—of being grabbed under the arms, of being dragged toward the car and forced to the floor in the back. The car then began to move, and in the few seconds when their hands were not upon her, when they had, as it were, given themselves time to congratulate themselves on her capture, she was able to determine that there were more than two men in the car (the actual number was always in doubt) and to identify them as Hawaiians.

The car gathered speed—she felt wind on her face—something, the top, was flapping. She began to reason with them, imploring them to take her purse and let her go. She tried to rise and was shoved back to the floor. A fist struck her on the cheek. Then another.

The faces above her grew shadowy. The car was now moving into an unlighted area, swinging into the driveway and the darkness of Ala Moana Park.

Such was the later graphic account of the troubled young wife who had left the Ala Wai Inn to escape a boresome party.

TWO

No one apparently had seen Thalia leave the Ala Wai Inn. No one had missed her. True, her husband, when questioned by Inspector of Detectives McIntosh of the Honolulu Police Department, some twenty-four hours later, stated that he had missed her between eleven-thirty and twelve o'clock—as near as he could judge for himself and on hearsay.

But it is just as likely that he actually missed her only after someone in that private dining room had said "Get Tommy!"

He had certainly not missed her a few minutes earlier when he had left their table to dance with another partner. He had left her seated there, and as far as he knew, or perhaps cared, she would still be there when he returned. Apparently, what Thalia did once she had accompanied him to this party, or any other for that matter, was her own affair. They went their separate paths of amusement. His were often to one or another of the other booths for a brief, boisterous reunion over a drink with cronies, or onto the dance floor with a partner who would be titillated by his amorous gallantries or touched by his sentimental recall of Southern memories. Moving past the podium that evening with his partner, he had asked the native orchestra to play "Pal o' Mine," a song to soothe any nostalgic heart.

Perhaps he too, in his way, sought the tender, personal bond that he and Thalia had never found with each other, an affirmation of his manhood which she did not give him.

Having told the Inspector that he had missed her,

Tommy related that he had immediately gone upstairs and made a complete search of each booth. Yet he then went on to admit that when he could not find her he "assumed that she had gotten a ride with other friends and gone home." It was something she frequently did when these parties began to bore and distress her. He did not mention the altercation in the private dining room or the slap Thalia had given a fellow officer. To tell of it would have caused some surprise on the part of the Inspector. He might even have wondered why Tommy did not pursue the search until he had found Thalia, or at least assured himself that she actually had got a ride home.

Instead it seemed that Tommy had gone back to the floor below with renewed zest and joined one of the officers with whom he had come to the party, one who was, at that moment, regaling a party of civilians with a rambling guide to submarine technology. Somewhat incoherently, for he had had a great deal to drink by that time, he was familiarizing his listeners with the operation of ballast tanks and submarine propulsion units, and dramatizing the act of submergence—using a shoe which he had taken off to visualize the submarine's underwater behavior.

Tommy joined in the discussion, apparently forgetting about Thalia. Then, at some point in that drunkenly solemn and esoteric discourse on submarines, Tommy's colleague found his speech too thick to continue. In attempting to rise, he fell and lay where he fell. Someone wondered out loud how long it would take him to surface after that deep dive into oblivion. Fellow officers, almost as drunk but still on their feet, surrounded the inert body. Gravely he was counted out. By the time he had been sobered up the Ala Wai Inn was getting ready to close. His wife had left with the other couple who were in their party, and it was Tommy who now drove his sick and only partly sobered colleague to the Manoa Valley home of another couple who had invited him to join them after the dance.

Before returning to his own home, Tommy, in what might have been a sudden surge of conscience or concern, called the house.

Thalia answered—but in a voice which he could barely recognize as hers. She was mumbling inarticulately, and he wondered whether she was drunk. He kept asking her to repeat what she was saying and finally he was able to distinguish the words. Something had happened to her. "Something terrible," he heard her say. "Come home!"

It was then close to 2 A.M., Sunday, September 13, 1931.

THREE

Lieutenant Massie had relied as much on hearsay as upon memory in stating that he had first missed Thalia between eleven-thirty and twelve o'clock. Thalia, who had never been sure of the time at which she had left the dance, was to recall at the trial of her alleged attackers that friends had seen her leave at eleven-thirty-five. For some reason, never clearly explained, one of these friends had happened to look at her watch. Yet, when Thalia was first questioned at about three-thirty on that fateful Sunday morning—by the same Inspector McIntosh who later questioned her husband—she said: "Around midnight I decided to go for a walk and get some air."

The factor of time, not then particularly significant, was to become much more vital an issue in the weeks that followed.

Time, as it happened, was significant that night to a Mrs. George Clark, a middle-aged, placid and rather motherly resident of the city, only because it was getting along toward twelve-thirty and she was tired and a little hungry. She and her husband, together with their son, George, Jr., had been visiting their neighbors, the Eustace Bellingers, across the way from their own home. They had spent the evening playing cards and rather than put her neighbors to the trouble of preparing refreshments, Mrs. Clark suggested that they all go to the Barbecue Inn in Waikiki.

The food was good and there was always a nice cheerful crowd there on Saturdays.

In the Bellingers' car they set out for Waikiki, only to find that the Barbecue Inn was overflowing with patrons. They decided then to try the Kewalo Inn on the Ala Moana.

In that first moment of seeing a woman in the beam of their headlights, standing directly in the path of their car and waving her arms for them to stop, Mrs. Clark caught some resemblance in the figure to her own nineteen-year-old daughter and felt a sharp clutch of fear. She even became momentarily convinced that it was her daughter, since the girl had gone out on a date that evening without saying where she was going. Immediately Mrs. Clark cried out to Mr. Bellinger to stop the car.

But as the woman came toward them, Mrs. Clark first felt relief because it was not her daughter, then concern because the woman looked hurt—her lips bleeding and swollen, an inflamed and angry bruise staining her right cheek.

"Are you white people?"

She spoke through stiff and barely moving lips . . . a glazed look of disorientation in her wide-apart eyes. When assured that they were white, she muttered: "Please take me home."

She had no purse. Her hair was down. She sat in the front seat of the car with Mr. Bellinger and the younger George Clark, not telling them who she was, answering their questions in brief, painful bursts of speech. She had been attacked by a gang of Hawaiians, she told them. She was forced into their car. Her purse was taken. She was badly beaten.

There was no hysteria in the telling, no tears, just the bald, brutal statements made with a kind of controlled fury—almost with an amazed resentment that it could happen to her, that anyone would dare!

The motherly Mrs. Clark urged that they take her to a hospital or the police. Her answer surprised them, for she was quite definite in telling them that she would go to neither.

"Just take me home please," she said. "My husband will take care of me."

Mrs. Clark, worried, solicitous, vicariously suffering the horror of a late night attack—seeing the dark savage faces of the attackers as they pulled her into their car and drove into the frightening, banyan-tree-shrouded gloom of the Ala Moana Park where no scream could be heard, where the worst of violent crimes was possible—could not resist asking whether she had been hurt in any other way.

The answer was an abrupt "No!" And then, because it was becoming much too painful to speak, she pleaded with them to ask no more questions, just to take her home.

Mrs. Clark was a little surprised, not by the request, but by the fact that although the woman's face had been badly mauled, she could see no other signs of violence. What she told the police later was that "we all noticed her evening gown seemed to be in good condition, and after reading of the assault, wondered how it could be if four or five men assaulted her"—for by that time the papers were all carrying the story of the rape of an unnamed naval officer's wife in the Ala Moana Park.

When the Bellingers reached Thalia's home on Kahawai Street in Manoa Valley, she assured them that she would be all right now, just thanking them and entering the house unaided, although there were no lights on and the house seemed to be unoccupied.

Her behavior—her adamant refusal of help other than being driven home—was somewhat mysterious to the Bellingers and the Clarks, but since it seemed that there was nothing more they could do, they then returned to the Ala Moana en route to the Kewalo Inn. A short distance from where she had been picked up, the younger Clark saw a purse lying in the road near the clumps of bushes which hedge the boundary of the park. He got out of the car and picked it up. Beside it lay a powder puff, lipstick, comb, and an empty coin purse. Later that night, on their way home, Mr. Bellinger turned these articles over to the police. They were Thalia's, of course.

There were some minor discrepancies in the statements which the Bellingers and the Clarks made to the police, but all were fairly sure that they had picked her up somewhere between four or five minutes of one o'clock on that

Sunday morning, or as many minutes after one. That margin of eight or ten minutes was hardly as important in the investigation which followed as was the twenty-five-minute difference between the time Thalia had first stated that she left the Ala Wai Inn (twelve midnight) and the time she stated at the trial (eleven-thirty-five).

FOUR

To his friends he was always Big Joe—Big Joe Kahahawai.
And he was Big Joe to the crowds who came to see him
practice barefoot football out at the Kauluwela playgrounds
or at Kamehameha Field where the big games were played.
"How's the toe?" he'd be asked. The toss of the head and
the wide grin would tell them that it was all honed up for
the big kick. That big right toe of Joe's—the care he took
in trimming the nail just so, to put the fine edge on its
contact with the ball—was as important to him as a
pitcher's throwing arm, a handball player's iron thumb.

Joe didn't do much else but play barefoot football. Oh,
he drank with the boys when someone else was doing the
buying. He'd play some pool in the Bethel Street parlors,
hang around lower Hotel Street watching the servicemen
going in and out of the Armed Services YMCA. Sometimes
he'd yell "Haole!" after them—a contemptuous epithet as
well as sociological classification.

At harvest time, if the need for cash became too pressing,
he'd go to work in the cane fields or on the pineapple
plantations, or he'd sign on for a few round trips on the
freighters which plied between the Islands. But he was still
Polynesian enough to cling to what anthropologists have
called the highest standards of leisure in the world. He
worked hard and long only when he saw some point to
doing so. Whatever he did had to have some socially satisfying reward to be worth doing. The National Guard to

19

which he had belonged for a time did not give him the kind of social satisfaction he wanted.

He was twenty four, just over six feet tall, a powerfully built, mahogany-colored pure Hawaiian, his massive, prominent-featured head held high on the thick, heavily muscled column of his neck. Sometimes, looking up at the golden statue of King Kamehameha I outside the Judiciary Building on the Iolani Palace Grounds, he would note the resemblance to himself in the features of the monarch they called The Lonely One. It gave him as much status among his friends as that prized big right toe. Not so much with his friend Benny Ahakuelo, also pure Hawaiian, who was an amateur fighter of some repute, and had been picked to represent Hawaii at the AAU championships in New York's Madison Square Garden the following spring. But among the others, his Japanese and Chinese friends like Horace (Shorty) Ida and Henry (Buster) Chang, it was a big thing.

Joe had practiced a little barefoot ball that Saturday afternoon—there was going to be a game the following day—and he was looking forward to visiting some calabash cousins that evening. There was going to be a wedding luau. He'd had no formal invitation to attend—calabash cousins weren't even related, it was something you decided you wanted to be—but once he was there, Hawaiian hospitality would see to it that he was made welcome.

But the luau, once the supply of beer began to run low, became a little less than amusing for Joe. He was short of money and he couldn't send out for more beer. It was a matter of pride with him not to stay when he could make no contribution to a family affair but his presence. And so, when Horace Ida, who had borrowed his sister's car that evening, suggested that they leave the luau and ride on out to Waikiki Park where there was a public dance, Joe readily agreed.

The dance that evening was sponsored by a local chapter of the Fraternal Order of Eagles. The pavilion was crowded. Despite its location in the essentially white district of Waikiki—or perhaps because of it—the dances there drew patrons from every stratum of Honolulu's polyglot and polychrome population. On Saturday nights the pavilion became, in a sense, the melting pot of Hawaii, in a kind of biological pull toward homogeneity which so rarely existed earlier in the week, or elsewhere.

Unlike the Ala Wai Inn, with its officer class patronage, a place where the music was subdued and Hawaiian, the Waikiki Park Pavilion had music which was ebullient, brassy, American. There girls came unescorted and danced with anyone—Hawaiian, Japanese, Chinese, Filipino, Portuguese—or with the Haoles or the enlisted Army and Navy personnel who were there. The economic level of its patrons was low; their enthusiasm for blending, as high as anywhere in the world during those few hours of unrestraint.

When money was short among friends, one or two would pay the price of admission, dance for a while then turn their re-entry stubs over to the others who waited outside. This was what Joe Kahahawai and his friends had done that evening—for, besides Horace Ida, he had been joined by three others, David Takai, also a Japanese, Benny Ahakuelo and Henry Chang.

The five of them had managed to get in a few dances before the pavilion closed at midnight, and Chang had enough money with him to buy a little more beer, enough to make them hope that the *luau* was still in progress at the home of Joe's calabash cousins and that the beer supply had been replenished, for it was toward the *luau* in the School Street district of Honolulu that they then set out in Horace Ida's car.

But there was no more beer at the *luau*, and the boys were not even allowed to enter the house. The party was drawing to a close and no one in the house wanted it revived. Benny Ahakuelo was dropped off at his home near Liliha Street, and the four remaining boys started homeward with Horace Ida driving.

It was at 12:37 A.M. on Sunday—roughly twenty minutes before Thalia Massie had been picked up by the Bellingers and the Clarks on the Ala Moana some two or three miles from that spot—that Ida's car narrowly missed colliding with a big Hudson that was crossing the intersection of North King Street and Dillingham Boulevard. Ida swung sharply to the right to avoid the crash as the Hudson swerved outward toward the center of the road with the same purpose. As the two cars came abreast of each other, the woman passenger in the Hudson—angered and frightened—screamed something at Ida about his driving. Ida retorted in kind and at once both cars stopped, their occupants prepared to continue the argument and fix the blame for the near-collision.

Had nothing further been said, had both cars continued on their way, the search for Thalia Massie's attackers might have ended after some vain attempts on the part of the police to find them, and the report of the attack quietly stored away.

But Big Joe suddenly came to life at this point, perhaps because he saw that the woman was Hawaiian and that the man with her was white. It was against the white man that he levelled his attack, yelling: "Get that damned Haole off that car, and I'll give him what he's looking for!"

The woman—her name was Mrs. Peeples and the white driver of the Hudson was her husband—at once got out of the car, ranting at Joe both in pidgin and in Hawaiian. Joe punched her in the face—he was no respecter of Hawaiian women who took up with whites—and was himself attacked by Mrs. Peeples, who struck right back at him, then, despite his height, made a grab for his throat. The entire episode lasted no more than a minute. Just as Thalia Massie, less than an hour earlier, had been prevented from continuing an attack on an officer who, she believed, had insulted her, so Joe Kahahawai was stopped by his friends from again striking out at Mrs. Peeples. They drove off.

Mrs. Peeples had no intention of letting it rest there. She had been assaulted by a native, a *kanaka*. As the wife of a white man she demanded protection. And so she told the police to whom she reported the incident a few minutes later, having had enough presence of mind to take the number of Ida's car.

Within minutes a call went out to radio patrol cars in the city to be on the look-out for a model A Ford, the license number of which was 58-895, and which was identified by the Motor Vehicle Department as a 1929 black Ford phaeton.

Fortuitously, the call was still being sent out periodically, and was also being given to officers who lacked radio communication with headquarters and called in from public telephones, at the same time that a call had just begun to go out concerning a criminal assault on a white woman in the Ala Moana Park area.

FIVE

Unlike the immediate awareness of being struck, of the instant pain which accompanies a blow, there apparently was a timeless period of separateness in Thalia's mind when what had happened, and the knowledge that it had haphapened to her, found no meeting ground.

Quite consciously, without hysteria, she could say, as she had said to the occupants of the Bellinger car: "I was attacked by a gang of Hawaiians. They dragged me into their car, took my purse, beat me up." But the other, that she had been sexually violated, of this she made no mention. Although later she was to explain her reticence by saying that she "didn't want it talked about all over town."

Alone in the house, after the Bellinger car had left, in solitude and a kind of safety, it seems that she was able slowly to accept what had happened—bewildered by it because with it there had been no accompaniment of pain as there had been with the blows, confused because she could find no tears. According to this account, she undressed and went to the bathroom, going about the practical business of cleansing herself of alien intrusion deliberately and methodically. Her mouth was on fire, blood had dried on her chin, her right cheek was discolored, and her lips were puffy and bluish. Her jaw looked twisted. This was so much more understandable than the other. This could fetch tears.

When Tommy returned, she was lying on the couch in the living room, wearing pajamas and wrapper, a handkerchief pressed to her mouth.

Only then, when she was able to put it all into words—
to tell him that she had been raped—did she cry, hys-
terically now, while Tommy stood transfixed, shocked, in-
credulous, at the same time feeling a mounting shame
because for an hour or more after her disappearance from
the Ala Wai Inn he had made no more than a perfunctory
effort to find her.

But whatever he felt was at once buried under a violent
eruption of rage against her attackers, a rage that gathered
into itself all the other rages for which he had never found
release.

In his solicitude for her at that moment, it seemed as
though the tender, personal bond which neither had found
with the other was, temporarily at least, available to them.

Tommy did now what Thalia had not done. He called
friends. He called the police. He was not going to shrink
from the clear duty of making public what Thalia did not
want talked about all over town. If she was sensitive to the
publicity, he was not. Her attackers must be found and
punished. His wife's honor must be avenged. Not that he
had any intention of taking the law into his own hands.
But to him, at this moment, Thalia was the innocent
young wife who had been ravished.

At a few minutes before three o'clock that Sunday morning, when city and county police had already questioned
Thalia at her home and had then taken her to the emergency hospital, Detectives Cluney and Black of the Honolulu Police Department, having been furnished with owner
identification and license number of the Ida car, drove
to the Ida home on Cunha Lane to pick up the driver.
This they did in response to the assault complaint lodged
against him and the other occupants of his car by Mrs.
Peeples.

Detectives Cluney and Black, whose car was not equipped
with radio, had been furnished the information in the
course of one of their periodic calls to headquarters. During
this call they were also told of the criminal assault on a
white woman in the Ala Moana Park area. There was no
immediate connection in the minds of either Cluney or
Black between the two cases. But in the mind of the duty
officer who was responsible for sending out the calls, a

glimmering of suspicion was already present, and he mentioned it to Detective Cluney when speaking to him.

Nevertheless, when Horace Ida was awakened early that Sunday morning and questioned by the detectives about the incident which had occurred at the intersection of North King Street and Dillingham Boulevard, the criminal assault was not mentioned. He was asked to describe the Peeples incident and to furnish the names of his passengers. Ida, a twenty-two-year-old Japanese who had recently returned from the mainland to be with his family because of his father's death, was at first reluctant to incriminate the others. But he finally gave the detectives their names and told them where all five had been that evening.

Ida was taken down to police headquarters for further questioning. It was then about 3:30 A.M. He was brought into the Detectives Assembly Room. In the adjoining office of Inspector McIntosh, Thalia was then seated with the Inspector, making a statement about the attack during which she again repeated that she believed her attackers to be Hawaiians. There were four of them, she said.

Ida, who was being questioned by another officer in the Assembly Room, an officer who was fully informed on what had happened to Thalia, and who too had already made a connection in his mind between the boys who had been involved in the assault charge by Mrs. Peeples and those who had raped the wife of a naval officer, asked Ida whether he had assaulted a white woman that night.

Ida, while admitting that "one of the boys hit the Hawaiian woman [Mrs. Peeples]," was vehement in stating that "we do not know nothing about the white woman."

That only two of the five were actually Hawaiian, and not all, as Thalia had believed, did not seem to be of much importance to the police. In the minds of many police officers that evening, the five were prime suspects. It was going to be fairly easy to prove their guilt.

SIX

There is an exhaustive, almost morbid, procedure in the investigation of the complaint of rape which, to the victim, can be as psychologically trying as the assault itself. The procedure is of course necessary, since, as is often the case, the charge may be either malicious or wishful. The use of force or violence in the assault, and the woman's non-consent, are key elements in substantiating the charge. In attempting to do so, the courts have always adhered to a doctrine which states that accepted standards of modesty and delicacy must be set aside in the interests of justice and truth.

And so it was that at about 2:30 A.M. that Sunday morning, Thalia was in an examination room at the emergency hospital. And there a young Chinese doctor, Dr. David Liu, having been told what had happened, followed the prescribed procedure in cases of this kind, knowing full well that in the event of prosecution he would be called as a witness.

That it was humiliating for Thalia there can be no doubt, since the concern of the doctor was as much in the interest of forensic medicine as it was in any injury, psychological or physical, which she may have suffered. She was, in a sense, a kind of pretrial exhibit.

Later, the doctor was in fact called upon to make a statement in the office of the City Attorney, and was asked whether he had made a pelvic examination of Thalia. He said, in answer that his examination indicated only an old laceration of the hymen. "No other abrasions or contusions noticeable. Patient was raped two hours prior to examination and she douched herself before she came into the Emergency Hospital."

He was then asked: "Doctor, could this woman have had four men and not show any marks?"

He agreed that this was quite possible. "One reason," he said, "is because she was a married woman. The vagina opened quite a bit."

This explanation did not seem to satisfy the City Attorney. He wanted to know more . . . wanting it confirmed more graphically in the interests of justice and truth, for he then asked: "She had a large opening and it was possible?" The doctor again confirmed that it was.

Not that there was anything prurient to the question. It was simply a conscientious application of the law's requirement which stipulates that penetration is an essential part of intercourse that needs to be established as an element of rape.

The nurse, a Miss Fawcett, who prepared Thalia for the examination was also questioned. She stated that she failed to see any indications of rape, that Thalia, to use the nurse's own words, was as "clean as a new pin."

At this point, the question of whether or not Thalia had in fact been raped was largely in doubt, for the doctor had found no evidence of seminal discharge in or about the genitals or on the clothing. But this cast no doubt on the credibility of the victim. Both the City Attorney and the police were quite sure that Thalia had been raped. It was only necessary to identify her attackers and prove it.

Lieutenant Massie, in his outraged determination to establish both the rape and the innocence of his wife, now found himself becoming a bystander in the matter. He had, without being fully aware of what he was doing, sacrificed the sanctity of his wife's body, of his and Thalia's lives together, to the public zeal for truth and justice, not knowing that his desire for it would stir a much greater public outcry that would diminish Thalia's role and in which he himself would become one of the leading figures.

To the police who came to her home in response to Tommy's call, then to the doctor and the nurse, and now to Inspector McIntosh at Police Headquarters, Thalia was endlessly repeating in words what she professed to have endured in reality. The questions she was asked hardly changed from one officer to another. What had happened? Where? How did you happen to be there? Why were you alone? Where was your husband? The same questions would be put to her later by the City Attorney who was to prosecute her attackers, and again by attorneys for the defendants when she was on the witness stand.

And in the course of all this questioning, especially in the questioning on that first night and in the two or three days following, small but significant changes began to show up in her answers.

Thus, she was quite sure at first that all the men in the car were Hawaiians, that she thought the car was old because of the sound of the engine and because the top was ripped and was flapping in the wind. Also, at first, she admitted that she would not be able to recognize any of the men except perhaps by their voices. She heard one name, she said. It was Bull. No, she did not get the number of the car.

Later, she became unsure of the fact that all the men were Hawaiians. The four she had thought were in the car became five or six. She did hear another name, "a common name like Joe." And then, by a remarkable feat of recall, she was able to remember the license number of the car as being something like 58-805. (The number of Ida's car was 58-895.)

During that first night while she was with Inspector McIntosh, Horace Ida, who was in the assembly room being questioned by detectives, was brought in to see whether she could identify him as one of the men who had attacked her. This was a surprising approach to the process of identification which usually occurs at a line-up in the presence of others. Thalia could not, however, recognize Ida at that meeting. Ida was wearing a brown leather jacket over his shirt when he was brought into the room. The following day, when she was again questioned about the identity of her attackers she was able to recall that one of the men had worn just such a jacket. She stated in fact that "she felt the texture of it."

In the course of that day, police picked up the four others who had been in the car with Horace Ida. Joe Kahahawai was taken from the playing field where he was about to join in the barefoot football game and placed under arrest. They were then taken by police officers to the Massie home in Manoa Valley, where both singly and in a group, they were brought before Thalia, who was asked whether she could identify any of them.

And now, following this almost-unprecedented identifying procedure, Thalia was able to declare that five men had attacked her, and that one of them, Benny Ahakuelo, had a gold tooth. Of the five, she identified four.

Police, in the course of that day, had examined the area of the Ala Moana Park where Thalia had stated the rape had occurred. They had also impounded Horace Ida's car. Customarily, the car would have been sealed and placed under guard in the impound area. Instead, it was driven to the area in the park known then as the old Quarantine Grounds, and pictures of its tire marks were taken by a police photographer.

It began to look as though there would be no lack of incriminating evidence when the five boys were brought to trial.

One reason for this uncommon diligence on the part of the police may have been that Tommy was a naval officer, and that shortly after breakfast that Sunday morning a vivid report of the rape had been telephoned to the Commandant of the Fourteenth Naval District at Pearl Harbor, Rear Admiral Yates Stirling, Jr.

SEVEN

It had always been deplorable to the Admiral to witness the changes taking place in the Islands over the years. As a young officer he had visited the Islands for the first time in 1892, when Hawaii was still an independent kingdom, only to learn a few months later that Queen Liliuokalani had been deposed and that Hawaii had become a Republic. This change did not affect the young officer as much as the fact that with each return to the Islands he began to see marked differences in the character of its peoples. The simple, picturesque Hawaiian culture which he had admired—its lithe, handsome and athletic people, who welcomed visitors with flowers and dance and song, whose hospitality with gift-giving made his visits so delightful— had rapidly been submerged in the waves of people who were being brought in to work on the plantations. Coolies, in his opinion, had overrun the Islands.

Now, at the height of his career, as the United States Navy's representative in the Territory of Hawaii, and as one who felt very strongly that Hawaii was America's Gibraltar of the Pacific, he was seriously concerned for the safety of the Islands whose population had been so thoroughly mongrelized. There were far too many orientals holding local government posts, he believed. He was not particularly enamored of the cult of the melting pot, as he called it, nor was he hesitant in making known his view that a larger measure of control of the Territory should be in the hands of the national government, that suffrage for the local population should be limited, and that on the ruling Cabinet of the Islands there should be a considerable proportion of high-ranking Army and Navy officers.

Nevertheless, he found much to be grateful for in his assignment to the post of Commandant of the Fourteenth Naval District. There was time for deep-sea fishing in a motor sampan, time to fly to the other Islands for pleasure as well as official duties, time to appreciate the natural beauty of the Islands and temporarily ignore its racial problems. It was in fact this beauty which was uppermost in his mind that Sunday morning when he was first informed of the rape of Thalia Massie. Into his appreciative reflections on cool trade winds and fragrant blossoms and coral sand came the shattering news brought to him by the Commander of the submarine base that the "kid bride of Lieutenant Tommie Massie, one of my officers, was criminally assaulted last night by a gang of half-breed hoodlums on the Ala Moana. . . . The police believe they have five of the criminals in the city jail."

From this report it was possible to gather that there might have been more. The Admiral was to say later that he had known Thalia as a friend of his daughters. She was a member of the younger set, he said, with all the qualities he could admire in his own children: attractive, quiet-spoken, demure, minding her own affairs. That such an outrage could be inflicted on this delicate girl whom he knew to be the daughter of prominent people and who had been raised in a cultured American home was unthinkable. And yet the Admiral, despite the stunning impact of this personal tragedy, was already thinking of the larger scene, of the men under his command to whom a woman's honor was sacred. Whether or not they knew her, she was a symbol of white womanhood whose desecration would rouse them to extremes of violence that were already fully developed in the Admiral's mind.

To avoid such violence, which at the very least would include the lynching of the five, orders were at once issued to stop all liberty. The Admiral was determined to give local authorities every opportunity to carry out the law. He would not interfere. As he himself explained, aggravating though the delay would be, he was going to be patient.

His patience however was short-lived, for within minutes,

accompanied by his shore patrol officer he was on his way to see the very authorities to whom he had intended to give every opportunity to carry out the law. Instead of displaying patience, the energetic Admiral confronted both the Mayor of Honolulu and the acting Governor and extracted a promise of quick and positive action from them. He saw to it that a message was at once dispatched to Governor Lawrence Judd, who was away visiting on another island, to return to Honolulu immediately.

He then called on the District Attorney for a full report of the case. And already, this veteran Navy officer—his years of command etched in the stern, weathered and uncompromising contours of his face, an officer who had always kept himself lean and fit, and in whose long upper lip, prominent nose and powerful jaws, one saw the strength and purpose with which he would demand obedience both of himself and others to a code—was beginning to have misgivings, for in his opinion the District Attorney was unfit to carry out the law. He was deaf. Furthermore, his assistant was young and inexperienced, the Admiral believed.

Incompetent, undisciplined, lethargic, diluted by oriental accretions . . . these were the regrettable qualities of Island government and law in the Admiral's opinion. How much more effective, how much sooner would the half-breed ruffians have been given the punishment they deserved, had his recommendations for national control been approved!

Failing this, the Admiral made it quite clear to the authorities that only by quick action, by punishment both adequate and speedy, could the prestige of Hawaii's white population be preserved.

In the weeks that followed he did everything that he could to make sure of both the punishment and the prestige.

Vicariously, he was leading the prosecution.

EIGHT

The cablegram which was delivered to Thalia's parents in Bayport, Long Island, a few days after the assault, may well have stirred a host of anguished and conflicting feelings in her mother, Mrs. Grace Hubbard Bell Fortescue. Apart from the immediate shock of its contents, it reminded her acutely of the fact that during the four years of Thalia's marriage she had seen even less of her daughter than she had in the years before.

How little closeness there had been between them! Whether or not it was what Mrs. Fortescue had wanted, they never shared the satisfying intimacy which should exist between mother and daughter. It seemed that there had never been time. Then with Tommy stationed at Pearl Harbor, what scant relationship existed had become more meager than ever.

The cablegram changed all that. In describing what had happened to Thalia, in telling of her admission to Queens Hospital in Honolulu where she was being treated for serious facial injuries, as well as for the possible consequences of rape, it created a compelling need in Mrs. Fortescue to be with her daughter. It seemed incredible that it had happened.

Throughout that summer Mrs. Fortescue had been participating in a local campaign for the repeal of the Volstead Act. From her headquarters at Roe's Hotel in Patchogue, Long Island, the town in which, four summers before, Thalia and Tommy had been arrested for taking a child from its carriage, this tall, slender, erect and patrician beauty, who looked far less than her fifty-odd years, had organized mass protest meetings, made speeches and launched broadsides against the evils of prohibition—all with the same fiery, if not so reckless, zeal which she had once displayed in campaigning for woman suffrage. Apparently she was neither deterred nor embarrassed by reminders of Thalia's arrest.

Now, all at once, this zealous, highly articulate and public-spirited woman found herself overwhelmed, her work disrupted, her dynamic approach to a problem or a cause paralyzed by a shattering and very personal calamity. She was consumed by a mother's painful solicitude for the daughter she had named, in the innocent and tranquil years before World War I, for the muse of comedy and pastoral poetry.

Accompanied by Helene, the youngest of her three daughters, Mrs. Fortescue departed at once for the Islands. Her husband, too unwell to travel at the time, went to stay at the Army and Navy Club in New York, one of the many clubs of which he was a member.

Mrs. Fortescue's father, Charles J. Bell, the President of the American Security and Trust Company, had once voiced the opinion—if one could be objective about one's own daughter—that had Grace been a man she would have been President of the United States. Now this aggressive, self-assured and determined woman, was embarked on the long, inactive journey to Honolulu, with concern for Thalia uppermost in her mind.

Who knows whether this strong-minded mother had failed Thalia in not providing her with a home of their own during the girl's childhood? Or Thalia's youthful marriage . . . had that been a mistake? There had been long periods when neither Mrs. Fortescue nor her husband saw anything of their children. But admittedly there had been plenty of reasons to justify these derelictions.

A long-time acquaintance has said that Grace Bell made a poor marriage when she selected Granville R. Fortescue as a husband, adding that she had practically supported him since their marriage. His income was always hit-and-miss. It was known that he had been involved as corespondent in a notorious divorce case during the course of which startling revelations had been made of scandalous behavior at U. S. Army bases, including the base in the Philippines at which Fortescue had been stationed.

For years, Mrs. Fortescue was forced to earn an income by giving bridge lessons in New York where she lived with her husband while their daughters were left either on her father's estate in Washington or at the summer place in Bayport.

Social and military distinction notwithstanding, it seems that money had always been a problem to Granville Fortescue, and whereas, prior to her marriage to him, Mrs. Fortescue had always associated with socially prominent people, after her marriage she avoided them. And this self-imposed isolation had continued until the death of her father, when a sizable inheritance made existence less difficult for her. Unfortunately, the change in her fortunes came too late to change the pattern of separateness between herself and Thalia. But now, dreadful though the reason for her voyage to Hawaii, it did give Mrs. Fortescue an opportunity to make up for all the years of neglect, an opportunity to be a real mother.

Harrowing days and nights of pain and indignity and terror both for Thalia and Tommy followed the assault. At first there was the operation which was necessary to mend Thalia's fractured jaw. It required the extraction of a tooth and the application of a wire splint to hold the jaw in place until it healed. Daily, as the jaw mended, a section of the wire had to be snipped off, a task which was undertaken by Tommy after Thalia's return from the hospital.

No one could doubt the torture she endured or the reflection of it as it was experienced by Tommy.

"When she swallowed, she almost screamed with pain," he was to say later, reliving it all as he spoke, his eyes clouded, his face haggard with remembered grief. "I didn't have much money, so I hired a day nurse and acted as night nurse myself. They gave me a pair of pliers and told me to cut the wires if my wife became sick. Otherwise she might choke to death.

"I tried to work, but couldn't. I kept seeing my wife's crushed face. I couldn't eat. I couldn't sleep. I was haunted by what happened to my wife. An abortion was necessary.

"It was worse than anything I could imagine. It had a strange effect on my mind. I kept hearing footsteps. I jumped up and ran out of the house but saw nobody. I used to get up and walk the floor . . ."

Now there was indeed a bond between them—of patient and attendant, if not of husband and wife.

During the time that Thalia had spent in the hospital there had been visits by representatives of the District Attorney's office, by the police, by naval officers from Pearl Harbor. Twice more, the five suspects were brought to her hospital room for identification. She had now seen them on at least three occasions, becoming more and more certain with each confrontation that these were the men who had attacked her . . . as certain as was Rear Admiral Yates Stirling, Jr., that these five "bestial, dark-skinned citizens of Hawaii" were guilty of the crime.

The arrival of her mother seemed to reinforce Thalia's conviction that these were the men. It was almost as though she felt impelled to produce the rapists as conclusive evidence that she had been raped, in a kind of gratefulness to her mother for having rushed to her side.

Yet, her mother's arrival did not achieve the rapport which both, perhaps, had wished for. Instead, within days, during which Mrs. Fortescue and her youngest daughter had stayed with Thalia and Tommy, Mrs. Fortescue rented a small bungalow on Kolawalu Street, a few blocks from the Massie home on Kahawai Street, but also in Manoa Valley.

The reason could have been given out that the Massie house was too small for them all, but it was not the real reason according to Thalia's Japanese maid.

Tommy's tormented description of what the days and nights were like after Thalia's return from the hospital notwithstanding, it seems that their quarrels were as frequent as ever.

"He swore at her and tell her to shut up. Sometimes she would walk out."

Thalia's relationship with her mother was not much better.

"She used to scold Mrs. Massie for not doing more work about the house, and sleeping less. Mr. Massie did not speak to her much, and these rows occurred so much that Mrs. Fortescue moved away."

Certainly none of this domestic tension could have been known to Admiral Stirling, for in describing both Thalia's courage and her mother's posture in the course of the trial he was to say that Mrs. Massie's story could not be shaken when she was on the witness stand and that her account of the crime was told bravely. Her mother's eyes, he said, never left her daughter's face. Her head held high, almost regally, her face impassive, "she revealed none of the awful bitterness that was in her heart."

The Admiral's predilection for the clichés of human emotion, for those which applied both to the righteous and to evildoers, was almost Dickensian.

Because of Thalia's illness it was not until the latter part of October that the Grand Jury returned a true bill against the five suspects. In mid-November, 1931, the case finally came to trial. By then, although the identity of the victim was still being withheld by the English-speaking press, the names of Thalia and Tommy Massie were as well-known to the citizens of Honolulu as the names of the suspects.

Admiral Stirling had demanded adequate and speedy punishment. To the Haoles of Honolulu there seemed to be little doubt that while punishment hadn't been as speedy as they might have liked, it was going to be adequate. Enough seemed to be known about the events of that night, as well as about the shady character of the non-Haole defendants, to convince them that these were the men and that they would be convicted.

Griffith Wight, the Assistant City and County Attorney, who was to lead the prosecution, had amassed an impressive portfolio of evidence against them. He was as certain of getting a conviction as were the mass of Haole sympathizers. He was going to be assisted throughout the trial by Harry R. Hewitt, the Attorney General of the Territory, and by two prominent local attorneys, Eugene Beebe and Frank Thompson. Nothing it seems was going to be left to the jury to do but listen to the evidence and bring in a verdict of guilty, thus assuring that the prestige of Hawaii's white citizenry, and especially of the Navy, would be preserved.

Yet a notable absentee during the major part of the trial

was Thalia's husband. Sea duty, it seemed, had taken precedence over his devotion to her and to the possibility that he might be called as a witness. To some it seemed that Tommy's departure for submarine trials in the Pacific at that time, was almost too convenient.

NINE

"I heard the name 'Bull' used, and I heard the name 'Joe.' I heard another name. It might have been 'Billy' or 'Benny' . . . and I heard the name 'Shorty.' "

In that extraordinarily comprehensive answer to a question put to her when she was called as the first witness for the prosecution by Assistant City and County Attorney, Griffith Wight, Thalia identified at least three of the defendants, this in spite of the fact that when she was first questioned after the assault, she stated that she had heard but one name which she thought was "Bull."

The trial had opened in the Judiciary Building on the Iolani Palace grounds on Monday, November 16, 1931, before Judge Alva E. Steadman of the First Judicial Circuit of the Territory of Hawaii. The few rows of seats in the public section of the courtroom were filled to capacity. Looking at the faces of their occupants one saw that these were the faces in the melting pot for which Admiral Stirling had so little use. They were as characteristic of Honolulu as the throngs which jostled each other during the lunch hour on the downtown streets of the city.

Representatives of the Navy were present in the role of amici curiae, although their presence was hardly as disinterested as the term implies.

In the row reserved for distinguished visitors sat Thalia's mother. Erect and intent she listened carefully to Thalia's testimony, following each word.

The first two days of the trial had been devoted to the selection of a jury. When the panel was finally completed,

it consisted of one Haole, six part-Hawaiians, two Chinese,
two Japanese and one Portuguese.

Its composition did not satisfy Admiral Stirling at all.
He would have preferred an all-Haole jury which would
have wholeheartedly agreed with his belief that the conviction of the five defendants was vital. Actually the racial
proportions of the jury were fairly representative of the
city's population. But this meant very little to a man whose
obsession with white supremacy had blinded him to all but
the desire for victory.

Although Admiral Stirling did not explain in so many
words just how this desire could be gratified, he kept wish-
ing that "the Territorial Government had shown more in-
clination to sympathize with my insistence upon the neces-
sity of a conviction."

The five defendants had engaged two Honolulu attorneys as their counsel. One was Judge William H. Heen, a
slightly built but agile and astutely observant counsellor
of Chinese extraction, who was both a Territorial Senator
and Chairman of the Senate's Judiciary Committee. The
other was the fifty-five-year-old William Buckner Pittman,
a brother of the Nevada senator, Key Pittman. The reputation of both these men as distinguished criminal lawyers
also distressed the Admiral. Before the trial opened, he had
urged Governor Judd to seek the services of the best legal
talent he could find to prosecute the case. He was sure that
both Heen and Pittman had been paid large sums by members of the native population to ensure the defendants' acquittal—an accusation which was angrily denied by both.
They had received no more than the nominal fees for their
services, they said.

There were other aspects of the case which displeased
the Admiral. He felt that important interests in the Islands
were anxious to prevent a conviction, since it might hurt
the tourist trade. Women visitors from the mainland would
stay away from Hawaii if they heard that there was danger
of assault by natives. The fact that funds promised by the
Chamber of Commerce to engage more competent counsel
for the prosecution were not forthcoming merely served to
prove his point.

In addition, as Tommy himself was to testify later, vile
slanders about Thalia and himself had been circulating in

the city. It was being said that they were on the verge of divorce before the assault, that there had never been a rape at all, that Tommy himself had beaten Thalia after finding her with a fellow officer. It was even being rumored that Thalia herself had invented the story of her rape in a search for notoriety.

The Admiral had begun to fear that in the circulation of rumors such as these the emotions of the races had been inflamed to a point where sympathy was on the side of the defendants. He already suspected that many members of the police force had been on their side from the beginning . . . and that malicious information had been secretly communicated to counsel for the defense. Under the circumstances how could a preponderantly non-Haole jury be expected to reach the right verdict?

In his determination to see that such a right verdict was reached, the Admiral warned the authorities that failing a verdict of guilty, a wave of violence might erupt in the city, that it might very well be expected from the men in his command, and that he doubted his ability to control them. He would have denied, of course, that he might have had a hand in fomenting such violence. He was simply saying that he would be powerless to stop it, and that, surely, was threat enough.

Indifferent to the Admiral's apprehensions, for they had enough apprehensions of their own, the five defendants, all in their early twenties, sat listening to the testimony of the white woman who, with the utmost assurance, was telling the jury that they were the men who had grabbed her, punched her in the face and dragged her into their car.

"Do you know which men got out of the car?" Griffith Wight asked her.

She answered promptly: "Yes . . . Chang and Kahahawai."

"Do you know which one hit you in the jaw?"

"Yes. It was Kahahawai."

She was just as explicit about what followed: "As soon as they dragged me into the car they started immediately. They were holding me in the back and I begged them to let me go. Whenever I spoke, he would hit me."

"Who?"

"Kahahawai. Chang hit me too. I offered them money.

I told them my husband would give them money if they would let me go. I said I had some money with me they could have. When I said that he turned around and said, 'Take the pocketbook'—and one of them took it from me."

It was Benny Ahukuelo who took the pocketbook, she testified. When she was asked how she recognized him, she said: "He turned around several times and grinned, and I saw his face. I also saw he had a gold tooth."

The five sat behind their counsels' table hearing the case being built up against them.

One sees them as they were then, typical of the restless, directionless Honolulu youth which had found no place for itself in the Islands. Some were the children of parents who had been brought to the Islands to work in the cane and pineapple fields. Some were the children of native-born Hawaiians or part-Hawaiians whose cultural patterns had been disorganized by successive waves of European and far-Eastern arrivals. Cut loose from their own traditions, too young to develop patterns of their own, they found consolation in mingling with others similarly adrift, similarly directionless.

Horace Ida, Japanese, round-faced, diminutive—his friends called him "Shorty"—of no settled occupation, sat listening to the testimony with an air of bland detachment. He had already denied any involvement with a white woman that night. All he had ever admitted to the police was that he was driving his sister's car when it was almost hit by the Peeples' car.

Beside him sat David Takai, also Japanese—lean, flat-featured, impassive. He was the only one Thalia had told the police she could not identify.

Henry Chang, Chinese-Hawaiian, solemn, curly-haired, more Polynesian-looking than Chinese, listened to Thalia with a kind of sullen curiosity thrusting through his solemnity.

Benny Ahakuelo, light-skinned, small-boned but muscular, looked rather sad, perhaps because his selection as Hawaii's representative at the AAU championship fights in New York was now very much in doubt.

Joe Kahahawai, darker, taller and much more powerful than the others, now sat with his back to the golden statue of King Kamehameha I. It was not the first time he had been in court, but he still seemed to be a little bemused by the experience, his wide mouth partly agape, his swart, massively featured head reaching with a kind of inarticulate anger toward the witness.

Not only by name but by their speech, by distinguishing features like Benny Ahakuelo's gold tooth, did Thalia identify them as she continued to answer the questions that were put to her. And as if that were not enough, she also knew what they had worn that night.

She could identify Horace Ida because she "felt his coat against her arm," the leather coat which he had worn when he had been roused from bed early Sunday and taken down to police headquarters.

Did she know how many of the men wore leather coats that night, she was asked.

"Just the one . . . Ida."

"Can you tell us how they [the others] were dressed that night?"

She answered: "Kahahawai had on a short-sleeved polo shirt, blue trousers. Ahakuelo—blue trousers, blue shirt. Ida—dark trousers, leather coat. And Chang—I think Chang, had on dark trousers."

Prosecutor Wight nodded his head. Rarely could an answer have been given him in such incriminating detail. He was naturally very pleased with it. He could now turn complacently to the identification of the car.

"Now, when these acts were completed [she had stated earlier that she had been assaulted four to six times], what happened then?"

By assault, as he had already made clear to both judge and jury, he meant sexual intercourse.

"One helped me to sit up," Thalia said. "He said, 'The road's over there,' then they all ran off and got away, and I turned around and saw the car. The back of the car was toward me . . . and I saw Ida get in the front seat of the car."

"Did you notice anything at that time?"

"I noticed the number."

"What was the number?"

"I thought the number was 58-805."

Surely that would seem near enough to convince a jury, since the actual number was 58-895, and it was understandable in the light of all that she had endured that a "9" might have looked like a "0" to her.

Naturally, it would have to be established that the car lights were on, permitting her to see the number on the license plate, just as it would have to be established that both the Ala Moana Boulevard and the Ala Moana Park were sufficiently well-lighted for her to distinguish the colors of their clothes. And this, Prosecutor Wight did, as definitively as he could. He did not want the jury's attention to wander—or their minds to wonder.

Now, having established that much, and having also established earlier that Thalia had left the dance at the Ala Wai Inn shortly after 11:30 P.M., September 12 because she was bored and tired of the party, he now asked her what she did after the attack, and where she went.

"I was very much dazed," Thalia said. "I wandered around in the bushes and finally came to the Ala Moana. I saw a car coming from Waikiki and ran toward the car, waving my arms. The car stopped. I ran to the car and asked the people in it if they were white. They said yes. Then I asked them if they would drive me home. They said they would, and I got on the front seat."

For reasons best known to himself, Wight had not asked her for how long she had wandered around in the bushes, nor how long she had waited before a car appeared. In fact he had asked very few questions connected with time. It was an omission that did not escape the attention of defense counsel, yet there was no doubt that it had taken courage to answer the prosecutor's questions.

Thalia's face, as she spoke, still bore the marks of the injuries she had received. Speech, because of her fractured jaw, was still difficult for her. She delivered her answers in a low, partly impeded monotone as though they were being wrenched from her only in the interest of truth. Prosecutor Wight found opportunity to tell the jury that she was crucifying herself on the witness stand "to protect the womanhood of Honolulu."

To the surprise of many, the *Hawaii Hochi*, a Japanese newspaper, did not hesitate to express its admiration for the "heroic fortitude" with which the very young naval officer's wife gave her testimony. It may even have mollified Admiral Stirling, who had been upset by the *Hochi's* bad taste in publishing Thalia's name, although it did nothing to change his opinion that their reports were slanted in favor of the defendants.

In the privacy of their home during the past weeks, Mrs. Fortescue was said to have scolded Thalia for not taking care of the house, for sleeping too much. Thalia's "rows" with Tommy were said to have exasperated her to the point where she had decided to move out of their home. But here in the courtroom, as she listened to her daughter's testimony given in the presence of the men accused of subjecting her to so shattering an ordeal, she could dismiss all the domestic strife as insignificant.

The case was being tried in full view of the public; the testimony would be read by thousands. Throughout her life, Mrs. Fortescue had always been at her best in the public eye. Feelings, beliefs, needs, were seemingly more important when there was a public with which to share them, when she could appeal to that public to witness what she felt, when she could call upon them to join her in any crusade on which she might be embarked.

Was it not conceivable that although she sat there listening in silence to Thalia's testimony, the public was aware of the courage and dignity with which she was sharing Thalia's ordeal?

Could it be doubted that she had already become, in the public eye, the tragic symbol of a mother's grief?

There was a quickening of interest in the courtroom when Judge William H. Heen rose to cross-examine the witness. The element of time which had been lightly touched on and then ignored by the prosecution, seemed to be very much on his mind. His voice, thin, high-pitched, his rapid yet polite, sometimes smiling delivery, were concentrated for long periods on time: on elapsed time and estimated time, on times of arrival and times of departure. He was responsible for his clients in much the same way that the control tower operator is responsible for the planes within his orbit.

"About what time was it you went to this party?"

"We went about nine or nine-thirty."

But Heen wanted a more precise figure.

"About nine?"

"Nine or nine-thirty," Thalia repeated.

Not satisfied, he asked her the question again, and again she said that it was nine or nine-thirty. But then he asked her whether it might have been *after* nine-thirty. Her answer was that it might have been; she did not remember the exact time.

Still he did not seem to be content with her answer, for a minute or two later, when she had told him that it was a drinking and dancing party at the Ala Wai Inn to which she had gone with her husband and two other couples, he returned to the question of time and asked her how she was able to recall that it was between nine and nine-thirty when they had left their home for the party.

She had begun to show signs of impatience with his persistent preoccupation with time. He was like a mosquito buzzing at her ear, brushed aside, only to return and buzz some more.

Her answer was intended to brush him aside. "We have a clock. I looked at it, and said it was about time we left."

The verbal slap failed to dislodge him. He returned to ask: "When you looked at the clock and said it was about time to go, what time was it according to the clock?"

"Shortly after nine, as I remember."

"About how many minutes would that be according to your best judgment?"

"I don't know—between nine and nine-thirty."

Now he stung her lightly: "But you said *shortly* after nine."

"I mean between nine and nine-thirty."

The sting had drawn blood. He was harassing her with this endless reiteration of what seemed to be a meaningless effort to pin her down. The questions were like drops of water being dropped on the same spot—boring into her skull. Would he never stop?

He did, only to resume at the point when she had left the Ala Wai Inn. At what time did she leave?

"It was about eleven-thirty-five."

"How do you recall that time?"

"Because some friends of mine left the dance at eleven-thirty and I left the party a few minutes after they did."

He did not call her attention to the fact that in her statement to Inspector McIntosh early that Sunday morning she had said: "Around midnight I decided to go for a walk and get some air." Whether or not he was aware of that statement, the rules of evidence would not have permitted him to introduce it. He hovered instead over her present statement. How did she happen to recall that her friends had left the party at eleven-thirty?

"My friend told me later that she had looked at her watch and it had been eleven-thirty."

"Several days later?"

"I don't remember."

"What is your best recollection as to that?"

"I don't remember."

"You don't know whether it was the next day or a week after?"

"I don't remember."

Failure to remember was the most effective weapon she could find against his onslaught, regardless of the effect such convenient gaps in her memory might be having on the jury. She could not even remember that she had left the Ala Wai Inn because of a quarrel with an officer in a private dining room, or perhaps this was the kind of thing that one would not talk about outside Navy circles.

There were a number of other aspects of her walk from the Inn that she could not remember. She did not know whether any of the stores were open on John Ena Road. She failed to recall whether there was any automobile traffic on that road. She had not noticed whether or not a dance was in progress at the Waikiki Park Pavilion.

What she could remember—and in great detail—were the traumatic events which followed her seizure by two of the defendants. She remembered for a positive fact that it was Joe Kahahawai who struck her, and that he was behind her when he clapped his hand across her mouth. She recalled clearly that it was he and Chang who pulled her into the car, and that there was enough light from a street light at the point where the car had stopped for her to see not only their faces, but to distinguish both the color and style of their clothes. She was even able to elaborate what she had told Prosecutor Wight. Henry Chang, she said now, wore a white or blue shirt with long sleeves which were rolled up. The shirt was unbuttoned at the collar.

Judge Heen seemed to be much impressed by such phenomenal powers of observation under the fear and stress and terrifying suddenness of the attack. Not that he disbelieved her or revealed any suspicion that these were observations which may have been furnished her later. On the contrary, he seemed only to be scientifically curious about these powers of recall, as one might be about the mirror memory by which some can make complicated arithmetical calculations at a glance.

In that curious frame of mind, he asked: "Now you stated that you saw Ida's face—or half his face. When?"

"While driving the car he turned to see what was going on."

"Was that the only time you got a glimpse of his face?"

Oh no, she had seen his face again later, she said, when he assaulted her.

"Did you see enough of Ida's facial characteristics at that time to enable you to identify him later on?"

"Well, I saw his—yes . . . I saw his trunk and part of his face. Of course his face was not unusual. I suppose if he had a brother that looked like him, I—maybe I would get mixed up."

But it seems that she was already "mixed up," for she had stated when first interviewed, that all the men were Hawaiians. Ida, by no stretch of the imagination could have appeared to be anything but what he was: oriental. Admittedly she might merely have meant natives when she referred to the men as Hawaiians, and apparently she was aware of this confusion in her own mind, for she now stated that she had known all along that he wasn't Hawaiian. She knew this, she said, because he had straight hair, thus adding a further physical characteristic to her armory of identifying testimony.

However remarkable Judge Heen may have thought these mnemonic feats to be, the element of time was still his major preoccupation. How long had it taken her, he wanted to know, to go from the Ala Wai Inn to the point where she had been seized by the defendants.

"I was walking quite slowly. I suppose five or ten minutes," she said, although she did not have a watch with her at the time, she added with a touch of the sarcasm which was so characteristic of her.

"Do you know," he asked her, "about how long it took the boys to take you from the spot where they picked you up to the place where they stopped?"

"It couldn't have taken more than two or three minutes."

But then, when he wanted to know how long the assault itself took, she could no longer play it his way. She was too dazed to know much about time then, she said. She lost all track of it. But what was happening in that span of timelessness was apparently unforgettable. She was not too dazed to know that Henry Chang was the first to assault her, that when she was assaulted by Joe Kahahawai he again struck her in the jaw. She said that when she started to pray, this infuriated him enough to strike her.

Judge Heen nodded gravely, sympathetically. How could one be anything but solicitous of a woman who had endured so shocking and revolting an attack? Yet, in spite of it all, in spite of her dazed condition, couldn't she perhaps estimate how long the attack had lasted? He wanted her to try and give a time.

Finally, though of course no one would hold her to it, she was able to say that it had lasted maybe twenty minutes before they let her go. Then it was Benny Ahakuelo, she thought, who pointed out the road to her where she "wandered around through the bushes and trees and finally came to the road."

In his pitiless preoccupation with time, Judge Heen now asked her: "About how long were you wandering around in the bushes and trees?"

But this she found it impossible to recall: "I was just beginning to realize what had happened to me and wasn't thinking about time."

Try as he might, Judge Heen could extract no more information from her.

TEN

Promptly, when counsel for the defense was finished with the witness, Prosecutor Wight rose to correct an impression that might have been left with the jury.

When had Thalia first mentioned the license number of the car to Inspector McIntosh? Was it before or after a police officer had entered the room and shown the Inspector a card on which the number was written down?

Naturally her answer could only be that she had mentioned the number before the officer's appearance. Had her answer been otherwise, the case might have ended there and then.

Though he might have re-examined Thalia on some of the statements she had made to defense counsel, Prosecutor Wight preferred not to do so. Surely Thalia had suffered enough at the hands of Judge Heen. It was her suffering throughout that would convince a jury, not the sly, unremitting attempt to discredit her testimony with cruel demands for chronometric accuracy.

He allowed her to leave the stand. Others would testify to what really counted—her suffering.

In minute detail, a naval surgeon described the extent of her injuries, produced hospital charts to verify the treatment she had been given, the high fever which had taken days to reduce. Then he told of the operation which had been performed on her to prevent childbirth.

No one would of course question the integrity of the doctor. Would it have helped Judge Heen to ask whether evidence of pregnancy had actually been discovered? He did not think so. At least he never asked.

Whatever the effect of the medical report on the jury, it was clear that in the minds of many who were in the courtroom it created sympathy, horror, fear. If these facts were true, then surely, they reasoned, Thalia's testimony to the effect that these were the men who had subjected her to so much pain, was also true. By a kind of emotional syllogism that had already swept through the Haole community of Honolulu, they seemed to reason from the premise that rape causes pain and suffering to the conclusion that these men were the rapists.

If there were minor lapses of memory in Thalia's testimony, surely it was because nature had mercifully chosen to help her forget. Defense counsel's questions were calculated to confuse her. They were third-degree methods of the worst kind. They had treated her as though it was she who was on trial!

It was in this mood of outrage that Mrs. Fortescue had listened to the cross-examination of her daughter. She sat there seething, barely able to listen as defense counsel called witnesses to discredit Thalia's testimony. She was sure they were lying . . . or they were testifying to statements of Thalia's which everyone knew could not have been accurate. How could they be when she was in so hysterical a condition at the time? Why mention them at all?

"I asked her if she knew the number of the car in which she had been abducted," testified Detective William Furtado, "and she told me she did not." He had been one of the first officers to arrive at the Massie home that Sunday morning in response to Tommy's urgent call to the police. "I asked her if she could recognize the boys, and she replied she could not recognize them, only by their voices."

Traffic Officer William K. Simerson, who had also come to the home, asked her whether she knew that all Honolulu cars had five numbers. It would help, he had said, if she could give him one or two of the numbers. But she told him that she could not. She could only remember that it was some kind of "an old touring car, either a Ford or a Dodge." She had told him she was positive that they were all Hawaiian boys, four or five—she wasn't sure. But she could not describe them.

A court bailiff, Frank Bettencourt, who had also gone to the house, testified that she could neither identify any of the boys nor give him any information on the license number of the car.

Earlier, when Thalia was being cross-examined by Judge Heen, he had asked her whether she had been questioned by police officers at her home that night, and whether she had replied to their questions.

She had answered then: "My husband told them, I think."

"Were you asked by them about what happened?"

"Inspector McIntosh asked me later on about it."

"Do you remember whether or not you told the officers about that night?"

"I don't remember," was the answer which had now become so familiar to the jury. "I wasn't thinking of the boys or the police . . . only about myself."

"Do you remember making a statement that you were unable to identify any of the boys because it was dark?"

No, she could not remember making any such statement, but now here were the witnesses to testify that she had done so. Granted her hysterical condition, it may have seemed strange to the jury, to say the least, that she could remember so much, and so little.

City Detective George Harbottle was called. He had come to the house that night with Detective Furtado. He was asked to corroborate whether or not Mrs. Massie had mentioned any names to Furtado.

"Well, Officer Furtado asked her if she heard any names," he said, "and she stated that she did not hear any names, but there was only one name that she remembered and that was the name 'Bull.' That is the only name she heard."

Leaving the witness stand, Detective Harbottle caught sight of Mrs. Fortescue staring coldly toward him. The expression on her face was one that he was to remember at a later date, and which, from that moment on, he was never likely to forget.

It was in the testimony of Inspector of Detectives McIntosh, called to the witness stand by the defense, that a revelation was made which dealt a resounding blow to the case for the prosecution.

The inspector had stated at first that he had driven the Horace Ida car to Thalia's home that Sunday following the assault to ask her whether she could identify it. She could not. It was he too who had arranged for the defendants to be brought to her bedside for the same purpose.

Now he was asked what he had done with the car thereafter. He made no attempt to evade the question but stated that he had driven the car around the area where the alleged assault had occurred. Apparently this seemingly deliberate maneuver to get something on the defendants hadn't worked. There were too many tracks of other cars in the area.

The Inspector was not asked why he had resorted to this stratagem.

Thalia's inability to recall having seen anything on John Ena Road did not discourage the defense. Whether or not Thalia had seen *them*, there were others who believed they had seen *her*.

George Goeas, a twenty-six-year-old Portuguese who was employed as an assistant cashier by the insurance branch of the Dillingham Company—one of the great Hawaiian enterprises founded by a stranded mariner who married into a missionary family and persuaded Hawaii's Merry Monarch, King Kalakaua, to let him build the island of Oahu's first railroad—came forward of his own volition to testify to what he had seen that Saturday night.

He and his wife had attended the dance at the Waikiki Park Pavilion and at the end of the last dance, at a minute or two before midnight, they had left the pavilion and driven their car a short distance along John Ena Road to the *saimin* wagon. The time was then, he said, about five or ten minutes after midnight. En route to the *saimin* wagon he saw a man and a woman walking.

"When I first saw them," he said, "she was on his right, about a yard in front of him. They kept that distance until they passed my car. Then I turned around and I looked back again and he just at that time took the opposite [position]. He walked about a yard in the front of her."

"How did you happen to turn around and look again?"

"I noticed the way she was walking at the time." Leaving the witness stand to demonstrate he said: "She was walking with her head on the side like this . . . and very stooped over, at a very slow pace like this, going down the road."

Both the woman and the man were white, he said. When he was asked how the woman was dressed, he said: "She had a green dress that came almost to the ground."

He was then shown the dress Thalia had worn that night. He said it was similar to the one he had seen the woman wearing.

His wife, also called to the stand, testified much as he had and also identified the dress.

Alice Aramaki, a tiny Japanese who worked in a barber shop on John Ena Road (Japanese woman barbers are as plentiful as man barbers in Honolulu), testified that she saw a white woman wearing a long green dress pass the shop at ten or fifteen minutes after twelve.

"What color hair did this woman have?"

"She was blonde hair."

"Was anybody walking near her at that time?"

"A man was walking. He was a white man."

"How was this woman with this green dress walking?"

"She was hanging her head down."

"How was she walking?"

"She was walking slowly."

Another witness, James Low, who had been to the dance that night in the company of three other men, saw a woman and a man on John Ena Road a few minutes after midnight. When he was asked how this woman was walking at that time, he said: "She—well, she was drunk, I presume it was. She was walking like a drunken person."

"How was her head?"

"Head down."

"And what kind of a dress did she have on?"

Mr. Low thought it was blue, but he could not tell her nationality, nor that of the man he had testified was with her.

In cross-examining him, Prosecutor Wight tried to discredit his testimony by getting him to admit that he had been convicted of gambling earlier that year, also by attempting to force a confession from him that he had violated the Mann Act and committed statutory rape. He admitted the gambling conviction, but denied the second charge. It was suggested by the prosecution that he had told someone that he did not want to testify against the five defendants because he expected to run for the Legislature in the Fifth District, where they lived. This, too, he denied.

To counteract the testimony of George Goeas, the prosecution produced a couple who testified that they were the man and woman Goeas must have seen on John Ena Road. The woman produced a green dress which she stated she had worn that night.

Perhaps because he was no longer available as a witness to the defense, George Goeas was not recalled to identify this couple, whose name was McClellan, but he was later to declare, at a time when his testimony could no longer serve any useful purpose, that he knew the McClellans well, and that they were definitely not the couple he had seen.

Not until the manager of the Waikiki Park Pavilion, Harold Godfrey, was called by the defense did the trial become less of a guessing game for the jury and more of a recital of evidence on which they could begin to form some valid conclusions.

At fifteen or twenty minutes after twelve, he testified, having been present in the pavilion when the last dance ended at eleven-fifty-five, he went to his car in the parking lot. Three or four cars, he said, were still parked in the lot. One of them belonged to a young Japanese whom he knew, Tatsumi Matsumoto.

The mention of the name did not seem important until Matsumoto himself was called.

Everyone knew him as "Tuts." He had been a student at the University of Hawaii, a grid star, financially independent, from an estate left to him by his father. Admittedly he had a weakness for hanging around prize fighters, and as he himself admitted, Benny Ahakuelo was his friend.

Driving an open Ford roadster, he had gone to the dance with Bobby Vierra, George Silva, and the latter's sister, Matilda. There was another girl with them, Alice Alves.

Cheerful, open, giving his testimony with an easy flow, he made one feel as though he were chatting with some fighter friends in the gym or in one of the Bethel Street bars.

He had known Benny Ahakuelo since "I am not sure just when. I first knew him about 1924—met him on the beach there; he lived down at Waikiki somewheres, you know? I am sure it was before the Fleet came in. I think the Fleet came in 1925 or 1924 . . ." He thought about that for a moment, then: "Just about the time the Fleet came in."

Had he seen Benny at the dance that night?

He had done more than see him. He had asked the same girl for a dance. "He was there asking for a dance, and I was asking her for a dance too."

His ingenuous narrative was so infectious that Judge Heen could not help asking: "Who won?"

He grimaced. "Neither of us won."

The rueful remark produced one of the rare moments of laughter in the court.

Now he was asked what he did when the dance was over.

"Well, after the dance was over we went out to the car there, and this Matilda Silva and Alice left with another party. They did not stay until the dance closed, and we met two other girls."

He left it to the jury to determine for themselves why Matilda and Alice had left. In a huff? Because the boys were more interested in other partners? Anyway, it was all in good fun, apparently.

"One was sitting in the car," he said, meaning one of the two other girls he had met, "that is, after the dance was over, but we were not sure if this other girl was going with us, so we waited for this other girl." He looked enquiringly at Judge Heen. "Shall I go on with the story?"

Judge Heen certainly wanted him to go on. He was not boring anyone, least of all the five defendants.

"We waited for this other girl, as we were not sure whether she was going with us or not. Well, she finally came on the car there and sat on the car."

The interchangeable preposition which might have confused listeners on the mainland was well understood in Honolulu. People often sat "on" the car, when they meant "in."

The girls sat alongside Matsumoto. Robert Vierra and George Silva sat on the rear of the car, facing away from the direction in which the car was going.

It was while they were driving homeward, Matsumoto testified, that one of the girls said to him: "Benny and them is following us."

At once, the prosecution moved to have the remark stricken as hearsay but by careful rephrasing of his original question, Judge Heen was able to establish that it was the Horace Ida car which was following them and that Benny Ahakuelo was one of its occupants.

Pretty soon, Matsumoto testified, the Ida car came up abreast of his, and at this point Bobby Vierra slipped off his car and leapt on to the running board of the Ida car.

Whatever his reasons were, Judge Heen did not want to hear them from Matsumoto—they would have been stricken anyway—and excusing Matsumoto, he now called Bobby Vierra.

Judge Heen understood these boys as the white prosecutor never would. He knew their origins, their behavior patterns, their records of delinquencies. He knew also that in an exchange of courtroom subtleties they would flounder. The careful build-up of an alibi was alien to them. They would tell what they knew. Had he believed otherwise he would never have called them, for in their very loyalty to their own, had they attempted to lie, the prosecution would surely have trapped them. In that sense, they were still the simple people Admiral Stirling had once admired.

Judge Heen asked him: "Who got on Tatsumi's Ford roadster when you came out [of the dance]?"

There were two girls, he testified. The name of one was Sybil Davis. The name of the other girl—she was Hawaiian —he did not remember.

"Who sat in the front seat?"

"Tatsumi driving, Miss Davis in the center, and the other girl on the side, right side."

He himself sat perched up on the back with George Silva.

"Now how about this car in which Bennie was on?" he was asked.

"They were following us."

"As you were coming down Beretania Street did anything happen?"

"Yes . . . Bennie tried to tell me something but I couldn't hear him and I told him to drive close. I tried to get on the bumper but the car moved away—came forward and back, and I told them to drive alongside and I got on the running board and I asked him what he wanted. He said 'Where you going?' and I said Judd Street. And then somebody asked me for a match—I don't remember who it was. We drove close to our car again and I got on."

He knew the others who were in the car with Benny, he said, but he did not recognize the driver. He had gone to school with Horace Ida, he said, but it was when they were young. He had been unable to tell that he was the same man—a statement which in its candor must have borne some weight with the jury.

George Silva corroborated Vierra's statement that he had left the car to jump on the running board of the Ida car, as did Sybil Davis.

"How did you happen to see Benny at that time?"

"He drove alongside of us and I turned around and I seen it was Benny," Sybil Davis said.

"Anything happen at that time?"

"Yes. Bob Vierra jumped on his car."

Margaret Kanae, the Hawaiian girl, testified that she was on "Tuts'" car, and that she saw Bob Vierra jump on Henry's car. By Henry she meant Henry Chang. He was apparently the only one in the car whom she knew.

"And then did he stay on Benny's car all the time?"

"No . . . he came back to our car."

There were others who had seen Benny Ahakuelo at the Waikiki Park Pavilion that evening. He was well enough known to fight fans to make his identity unmistakable.

A Mr. William U. Asing, Chief Clerk at Honolulu's Board of Health, testified to seeing him at the dance at about eleven-forty-five . . . "and again after the dance was pau . . . [over]."

His two companions that evening, Agnes and Alice Kam, had also seen Benny at the times stated by Asing.

John Puaaloa testified that he had left the dance hall at eleven-thirty and had seen Henry Chang outside the pavilion entrance. Chang called to him and asked him for a stub.

"What kind of stub was that?"

"Return stub to get back in the dance hall."

"Did you give him the stub?"

"Yes."

Despite the testimony of so many witnesses who claimed to have seen one or more of the defendants at times which would have made it impossible for them to have been Thalia's assailants, Griffith Wight, in his closing argument for the prosecution, clung to Thalia's statement that she had positively identified four of these "lust-sodden beasts." Save for a single digit, he said, she had identified the license number of the Ida car. Moreover, whether or not there were the tracks of other cars in the old quarantine grounds where the rape occurred, the tracks of that car were also seen. That Inspector McIntosh had driven the car around the area did not seem to disturb him at all.

The defense in its closing argument pointed out that the Honolulu police department had employed identification procedures which most police forces had discarded half a century ago. On three different occasions they brought the defendants before Mrs. Massie and as good as told her: "These are the boys we suspect, and we want you to identify them."

It must have been known to the jury, as it was known by experienced officers, that Hawaiians will talk. Confessions were usually secured from them with very little difficulty. If the accused were guilty of the rape, this would be the first time in the memory of many officers where one or more of the accused hadn't confessed.

The jury retired to consider their verdict after having been reminded by the bench that "under the laws of the Territory of Hawaii [since modified], a female who is alleged to have been raped, is a competent witness in the prosecution thereof, but no person shall be convicted of such an offense under the mere testimony of the female, uncorroborated by any other evidence or circumstances."

It was a question now of whether or not Thalia's sole testimony had been corroborated. In their statements to the police, the defendants had all denied being in the

Ala Moana Park that night. They had driven straight from the dance toward town, their presence en route having been testified to by Matsumoto and his friends. They had returned to the *luau* for a few minutes, and then, at 12:37 A.M. their car was in near-collision with another car at the intersection of North King Street and Dillingham Boulevard.

Time must have preoccupied the jury as they sought to separate fact from fiction, much as it had Judge Heen. They were not so much concerned with whether Thalia had actually been raped, but whether in the elapsed span of minutes as testified to by Thalia—at the times stated by witnesses both for and against the defendants—the five youths could have been the rapists.

There was no decision on the first day. On the following day, the jury asked that some of the testimony be reread to them. Later that day, sounds of bitter quarreling were heard coming from the jury room. It was said that some of the jurors had almost come to blows and that Judge Steadman had found it necessary to enter the jury room to make peace.

For four whole days, the defendants waited for the jury to arrive at a verdict. It was reported that in the course of that time the jurors had polled a hundred votes. Finally, at the beginning of their fifth day of deliberation, the foreman sent a note to the Judge. The jury was unable to reach a verdict, it said. They had never come closer than seven to five for acquittal. It was hopeless to go on.

Judge Steadman dismissed the jury. The defendants were released on bail to await a second trial.

The non-Haole community of Honolulu was up in arms. The defendants should have been acquitted! Quite the contrary, raged the Haole community. As Admiral Stirling and other spokesmen for the Haoles said, the defendants' reputations should have been enough to convict them. They were simply not deserving of the reasonable doubt which had clearly made it so difficult for the jury to bring in a verdict of guilty. "Everyone knew they were guilty," the Admiral was to say later. But what he seemed to be saying was that given a little less law and a little more forcefulness, the five would have been clapped into Oahu Prison for the rest of their lives.

Mrs. Fortescue agreed with him. It was unthinkable to her that a jury would dare to question their guilt—doubt Thalia's testimony. There was no thought in her mind now of returning home. She would stay until Thalia's ordeal had been avenged.

ELEVEN

Before her arrival in Honolulu, Mrs. Fortescue's notions of the Islands had been largely confined to the tropical paradise view. Now, in less than a month, so many trying days of which had been spent in a dingy Honolulu courtroom, seeing her daughter divested of all dignity, hearing her testimony contradicted and distorted by native witnesses whose contempt for white people was all too obvious to her, she had fallen prey to the same disenchantment that had taken Rear-Admiral Stirling half a lifetime to experience.

As one contemptuously wistful writer put it, reflecting Mrs. Fortescue's feelings in the aftermath of the trial: "The simple, pure strain Hawaiian has virtually disappeared, swallowed up by the evil influx of polyglot scum and Eurasian riff-raff whose vices threaten to turn the isles of innocence into a seething inferno."

That writer was not only contemptuous. He was also scared. So was another, who wrote: "The snake has entered our Pacific paradise!"

Mrs. Fortescue had no doubts about espousing this point of view. It was fuel for her own "seething inferno."

"Unless you want to believe that this girl is an unmitigated liar," Prosecutor Wight had appealed to the jury in his closing argument, "you must accept her immediate identification of two of the defendants . . ." not to mention two of the others whom she had identified *in flagrante delicto*, as it were.

A majority of the jury had, however, chosen to believe

that her identification of the men was dubious, to say the least.

It was only too easy now for Mrs. Fortescue to go along with Admiral Stirling's emphatically stated opinion that with a Hawaiian jury, composed largely of Asiatics or men of mixed blood, conviction in a case of this kind, was impossible.

The injustice of it, the cynical disregard for honesty, the malevolent devices employed by the defense to prove that Thalia had lied and that her identification of the men was not her own but had been suggested to her, roused Mrs. Fortescue to a fury of resentment and anger against a community which would allow such flagrant irresponsibles to scoff at the law.

Like a hospital patient who learns to his relief that his sickness is not unique, Mrs. Fortescue now began to discover that there were many who were only too ready to furnish her with abundant evidence of the "Hawaiian sickness," the Asiatic scourge.

Rape was all too frequent a crime in Honolulu, she was told. The guilty were rarely punished. Even when guilt had been proved beyond a doubt, the mildness of the sentence mocked the Anglo-Saxon code. It openly defied one of King Kamehameha's earliest laws. Women, children and the infirm, stated the law, shall be safe on the highways of Hawaii.

The prosecution had not neglected to remind the jury of that law. But they, the Asiatics and half-breeds, had laughed at it. Just as the non-Haoles had laughed at the efforts of Honolulu's white women to bring about reform. Through their Citizens' Organization for Good Government, they had made a survey of rape cases in the city. Bitterly they came to the conclusion that it was always the woman who was put on trial, the woman alone who suffered. The native defendants went about their revolting business, safe in the knowledge that they had little to fear.

There was a kind of bitter satisfaction for her in reading an editorial which had appeared in the Honolulu press the previous year:

The ravishing of defenseless women and girls is not going to be confined to Kakaako and Tin Can Alley. It is going to extend to Waikiki, to Manoa . . .

Yes—it had reached lovely Manoa. The editorial went on:

Honolulu is certainly going to see a revulsion of feeling in the community which will gravitate into lynch law and killing.

Dire warnings of this kind created a clangor of familiar bells in the mind of Mrs. Fortescue.

Here was a Cause! It was much more personal and emotionally affecting than others to which she had devoted her energies. Suffrage for women, the repeal of Prohibition, these were hardly more than mental exercises compared to the immediate need for the protection of women against rape, for laws that would suppress, not virtually condone; and above all, for Thalia's vindication.

She could now, as a woman with a very personal stake in reform, bend her mind and her powers toward seeing that when the defendants were again brought to trial, they would be summarily convicted.

She was not alone in this determination. Navy personnel were infuriated. Rear Admiral Stirling expected to hear any day that "one or more of the defendants had been found swinging from trees by the neck up Nuuanu Valley or at the Pali." He had warned the Governor that it might happen.

His words could hardly have been more prophetic, for on the Saturday night immediately following the end of the abortive trial, a pack of men (who may have been Navy men, the Admiral later admitted) seized Horace Ida and rode up with him to the Nuuanu Pali.

Provocation for the act had come, it was said, when a note was received at the Navy Yard, addressed to the Petty Officers' Mess at the Submarine Base. Why it should have been sent there was a mystery, if indeed it was ever sent and not composed by Navy men themselves. It read: "We have stolen your money, we raped your women and we'll do it again. You're a lot of yellow cowards, navy men." It was signed "The Kalihi Gang."

The note, in spite of the fact that the language in which

it was couched was hardly that which natives would use, and also despite the fact that "gangs" as such, are not characteristic of Hawaiian youth, was all that Navy personnel needed.

That Saturday night, street fighting began almost as soon as the men had streamed from the base and entered the city. They had come prepared for trouble, wearing dungarees rather than uniforms, roaming the streets in belligerent packs. They were going to give the kanakas a taste of Navy might—just a sample of what would happen if those five rapists weren't thrown into jail pretty damn quick.

Admiral Stirling had issued a warning to all naval personnel to conduct themselves in a manner that would permit the law to take its course. He threatened them with severe punishment if they acted otherwise.

The warning went unheeded. Or perhaps it was taken as a challenge. On the narrow, dusty streets of downtown Honolulu, on Bethel and Hotel, on Likelike and Mililani, the packs pounced indiscriminately on any young natives they found. The vengeance squads marched through the streets surrounding Honolulu's ancient mission houses where the missionary forebears of so many of Hawaii's contemporary white families had conducted religious services for the natives, taught them to read the Bible and sing hymns, where they sewed shapeless dresses to cover the native women's nakedness. The squads had more violent teaching methods in mind.

Soon the word spread through the native quarters that the Navy was making pilikia, trouble. Now the native packs began looking for Navy men.

In the course of the evening the police answered a dozen riot calls, breaking up fights in bars, pool halls, amusement arcades.

Urgent appeals to the Navy to round up their men who were making the streets of the city unsafe for any non-Haole brought the reply that the only people who were unsafe in the city were white women. It was the wild, native hoodlum element which was to blame for the riots.

The police could not handle the rioting packs, thus proving Admiral Stirling's contention that they were incapable of dealing with native disregard for law and order. There were too many natives and orientals on the force anyway, he said.

Horace Ida was out driving around that night with a friend. That he, or any of the other defendants, was out on bail at all was another aggravating cause of the trouble, said the Admiral.

His car had apparently been trailed from his home, for on Kukui Street where a lot of the street fighting was taking place, he became aware of the fact that his car was being followed.

On the traffic-jammed street it was impossible for him to get away in his car. He did the next best thing. He left his friend in the car and jumped out, hoping to lose himself in the darkness. But the others were already out on the sidewalk as he stepped from his car. Five men closed in on him. A gun was thrust into his back. He was marched back to their car which now swung mauka toward the mountains and sped up to the desolate heights of the Nuuanu Pali. Four more cars had suddenly appeared, following the first, roaring up the steep winding road to the summit.

Near the summit, the cars turned off the road into a fallow cane field, forming themselves into a semicircle as they stopped and their occupants piled out. There were at least a score of them. They encircled Ida. The gun was now at his head. The men wanted the truth about the rape. He'd talk or have his brains blown out. In a constant pressure, the white men's voices demanded confession. Who went first? Was it you? Big Joe? Chang? Where was she sitting, front or back? Who sat next to her?

They quoted and misquoted testimony in the trial which apparently all had read . . . or misread.

They already had Benny Ahakuelo, they told him. Benny said the whole thing was Ida's idea. True? Come on—let's have it! The truth!

He could only deny and deny . . . and yet again, deny.

They ripped the sweater from his back, tore off his shirt. Now their heavy leather belts were swinging at his body, buckles tearing into his flesh. He fell to the ground and lay still. They began kicking him.

Suddenly he was screaming—howling in an agony of pain and terror—an almost-insane and hysterical release of torment that made them stop short of the lynching that might have been the next step. They left him there.

The following day when he lay in bed, hurting and bandaged, he learned that the same pack or another had called at Benny Ahakuelo's home that night. His absence saved him from a similar attack or worse.

Ida accused the Navy of being responsible for the attack on him. The Navy promptly produced men who seemed to answer to his description of them, but Ida could identify none of them.

Nonetheless, the English-speaking press now published a story to the effect that Ida had confessed to the unidentified men. The story went that when he was asked whether Thalia was in the front seat with him, he blurted: "No—she was in the back seat with Kahahawai."

Neither the paper's informants nor the attackers themselves were ever identified, and since the men to whom he was said to have made this dubious confession never came forward, the authorities could make no use of it. In Haole circles however, it was accepted as valid confirmation of what they already knew.

The sensational rather than authoritative Honolulu Times devoted its next issue to the "Shame of Honolulu." Thousands of copies were mailed by naval personnel to the mainland. Its lurid accounts of conditions in Honolulu were reprinted in the mainland press. Honolulu, was its repetitive lament, was unsafe for women!

When Admiral Stirling was asked by the Governor to make a public denial of this slander, he refused. It was true, he said. Until more effective protection could be provided by the police, until there was drastic reform in the constitution of the police force, he would continue to announce publicly that Honolulu could not provide protection for tourists from the mainland. It was an opinion that was now shared by Acting Secretary of the Navy, Admiral Pratt, who not only expressed his concern to the Governor, but authorized Admiral Stirling to take all necessary steps to protect both Navy men and women from the native hoodlums.

Larger shore patrols were immediately established, both foot and mobile. Admiral Stirling demanded that the members of these patrols be given the same authority as police to shoot to kill without being tried for murder by the civil authorities.

He denied that the Navy was attempting to dominate the community by this measure. Martial law was the last thing he wanted; but the Admiral, it seems, was protesting too much.

He gave his wholehearted approval when Navy wives began carrying pistols in their purses. What splendid courage they displayed when they challenged each other to pistol matches on the beach—combining Waikiki with watchfulness, as it were! What a pity that a member of one of his patrols happened to seriously wound a native fisherman one night!

Although it would have shocked the Admiral to be told that he was whipping up a vindictive storm, his indignation with the weak authorities who had failed to heed his warning was having its inevitable effect on the Haole community. They were so few, and the natives were so many. Honolulu was aswarm with these lust-sodden beasts, a term which was fast becoming generic for all non-Haoles.

It was having the same effect on Mrs. Fortescue, not that she needed much encouragement to fear for the safety of Thalia and for her younger daughter, Helene.

She had heard that friends of the defendants were going to try and frighten Thalia into leaving the Islands. Without her testimony, no retrial would be possible.

She had also heard that Ida's supporters might take retaliatory measures for his beating by bombing the Massie home.

With Tommy still away on sea trials, she persuaded Thalia to stay with her and Helene at her bungalow on Kolawalu Street. The Navy dispatched an armed patrol to guard both houses.

Yet, reassured though she was for the moment, she felt sure that something was bound to happen. The terror would not cease. The fear of rape was in the air like a lethal gas. It was a conversation piece at women's luncheon parties and club meetings. More dangerous were the lying stories about Thalia's character which were so sympathetically relayed to her. Surely, she kept telling herself, there had to be a way to put an end to them.

In this determination she was backed by Admiral Stirling,

who also sought a way. He wished for anything which would give him reason to act, to bring the five defendants to justice.

He was as much dismayed as she was when he learned from the Attorney General's office that the retrial would probably be postponed until after the Fleet's February maneuvers, unless of course some new evidence could be found against the five men.

The Admiral threw up his hands. Where was this new evidence to come from? Did they not have evidence enough?

For Mrs. Fortescue the need for new evidence was like a call to action. It would be a way to put an end to the terror.

TWELVE

Mrs. Fortescue had no well-ordered plan of action. It was hard to be clear-minded when she was burdened with fear for Thalia's life, with constant concern, since his return, for Tommy's sanity. The whispering campaign with its insidious suggestiveness was having a destructive effect on his self-control. He was sullen, uncommunicative, restless and frustrated.

In desperation, Mrs. Fortescue called on Judge Steadman, who had presided at the trial of the five men. Why could they not be imprisoned until the retrial? She feared that they would not stop at murder to prevent that trial. Their very presence on the streets was an incentive to violence for their supporters. She had heard, she told the Judge, that they were boasting openly that they would never be convicted.

The Judge agreed with her that the men were unquestionably a menace. He had even suggested to their attorneys that the men themselves would be safer in prison, in view of the attempts by Navy men to force confessions from them, ill-advised though these attempts were. Regrettably, the men's attorneys did not see it the judge's way.

Bail for the five had been set within the limits they could be reasonably expected to meet. That was the law. There was nothing more he could do about it. He had, however, imposed one restriction on their liberty. They had been ordered to report to the Judiciary Building each morning, pending preparations for the new trial. He would have the power to imprison them only if they violated that order, but so far there had been no violations. They had reported regularly.

As for the date of the new trial, the Judge was as much in the dark about it as she was.

The authorities were disinclined to change their decision to postpone the trial until after the visit of the Fleet; this, in spite of the fact that Admiral Stirling had personally made repeated requests both to the Governor and the Attorney General to expedite it, if only out of compassion for Thalia and Tommy Massie. Had Thalia's testimony not been indispensable in the retrial, he would have ordered Tommy's transfer to another station forthwith.

There was a reason other than the Fleet's visit which, Mrs. Fortescue learned, may have been instrumental in delaying the retrial. This she discovered in discussing the matter with the clerk of the court, a Mrs. Whitmore. If the jury were again to disagree, she was told, the men would automatically go free. Hence, the prosecution was reluctant to bring the case to trial until they were sure of getting a conviction.

Mrs. Whitmore, who did not seem to be averse to discussing the case with Mrs. Fortescue, admitted that "the defense so effectively riddled the prosecution and nullified the known evidence that it will be practically impossible to bring about a conviction unless one of the defendants confesses."

Without perhaps realizing it, she was as good as saying that the jury should have brought in a verdict of acquittal; but this was not how Mrs. Fortescue read her remarks. She read them as native trickery, as prejudice against the whites.

But there was one thing the defense could never nullify, and that of course was a confession.

Confession became the touchstone of Mrs. Fortescue's thinking, following her talk with Mrs. Whitmore. The word, as she herself was to admit later, rang in her brain!

She began to develop a kind of conspiratorial approach to the problem. She would have to fight cunning with cunning. It seemed to her that there was no other way in this city of dark and threatening menace, where there was a kind of "Nights in Chinatown" atmosphere, where white women took their lives in their hands to walk the streets after dark, where Asiatics gathered in their dens to plot the destruction of the white man.

But she was also afraid. Her fear became near panic when she learned of the escape of two prisoners from Oahu Prison on New Year's Eve. One, a murderer serving a life sentence, was reported to have been seen in Manoa Valley. This did not alarm her so much as the fact that the five defendants might seize this opportunity to kill Thalia and blame the escaped convict for the murder. To her it would be the same kind of cunning which their attorneys had employed in "riddling the prosecution."

By the following Wednesday, with the escaped man still at large, Mrs. Fortescue's fevered and frightened imagination had begun to creep toward a plan which would match their cunning with cunning of her own. It was not the well-ordered plan which she may have been looking for, but the more she thought about it, the more daringly possible to her did it become. It was so much in keeping with what had happened. It belonged in a city like Honolulu. On the mainland it would have been impossible. Here, it would work!

Excited, her mind already fixed on its successful outcome, she hastened early that morning to confer with Tommy before he left for the base.

Thalia was still asleep. They spoke in whispers. Persuasive, eloquent, obsessed by the determination to see the five alleged rapists punished, her daughter vindicated, she told Tommy her plan. If it was dangerous, was it any more dangerous than their present condition? If it was illicit, was it any more illicit than the methods of the defense in that first trial? They had everything to gain, nothing to lose. In the eyes of the non-Haoles they had already lost. But now they would turn the tables!

By the time Tommy left for the base, preparations for putting the plan into action were in full swing.

Cunning was the theme of the plan, no different from the oriental cunning of the five men's defender, the man who had so humiliated Thalia on the witness stand, made her the defendant. The world would learn now who the guilty really were. Cunning was the plan's theme; deception was its handmaiden.

Deceptively concerned, Mrs. Fortescue appeared at the

Judiciary Building that morning to inform the clerk of the court of an alarming event. Two of the defendants, she had heard, had provoked their own arrest on another island in order to obtain jail protection. Did the clerk of the court know whether it was true? The clerk of the court summoned the court probation officer. It was not true. The men, all of them, were reporting regularly. One of them, Joseph Kahahawai, had in fact reported in just a few minutes earlier. Eight A.M. was his appointed time.

The big Hawaiian? Yes, Big Joe. Well, it was a relief to know . . .

She thanked the probation officer and left.

Joe Kahahawai. She had seen him in the courtroom almost every day for three weeks. Would she recognize him if she were to see him again? She had never really looked at any of their faces. They appalled her. But now she would have to make sure.

In her small roadster, she drove to a newspaper office and secured copies of all the defendants' pictures. She also learned Kahahawai's address. Then, having studied a map of the city at the library, she drove to the area—"a tenement house rabbit-warren," as she later described it. It was hardly the right place for the execution of her plan, located as it was in the heart of the enemy camp.

Tommy was waiting for her when she returned home that afternoon. The plan had excited him to the point where he could hardly wait to put it into effect. What was the next step? Mrs. Fortescue told him what she had so artfully learned at the Judiciary Building that morning. Kahahawai reported in daily at 8 A.M. Then he was the obvious objective of the plan. There were other good reasons for the choice. Tommy had heard rumors that he was getting ready to crack. He had also heard that the big Hawaiian had confessed the rape to his father. Unlikely though it was that such a confession, had it actually been made, would be known to anyone else, this tale confirmed Mrs. Fortescue in her feeling that Kahahawai was the right choice. But they would have to be sure that the information she had received at the Judiciary Building that morning was correct.

Next morning, she again visited the Judiciary Building. She parked her car across from the entrance, and waited.

She had pinned Kahahawai's picture to the lining of her purse. From time to time, as she waited for him to arrive, she studied it. How loathsome it was, that leering face! The mere sight of it was enough to overcome any doubts she may have had about the rightness of her plan.

By ten-thirty, when there was still no sign of him, she was forced to leave. A luncheon party to which she had invited some friends, had to take precedence over her vigil.

It was hard making polite conversation with guests when there was so much on her mind, when she had to be sure she let nothing slip. She would have loved to be able to let them in on it, knowing how they would have all approved. Later, when it was all over, they would understand why she seemed so preoccupied that afternoon, why she was not her customary superb self at playing hostess to them.

When Tommy arrived that afternoon, he was accompanied by two Navy enlisted men, seamen he could trust implicitly. He had confided the plan to them and asked for their help. They had agreed to join him. One, Albert L. Jones, was known to Mrs. Fortescue. He had been a member of the armed patrol which had guarded Thalia during Tommy's absence at sea. He was a veteran Navy man, a Southerner. There was something reassuring in the opinions of this wiry, hard-eyed and experienced sailor. His fondness for the native drink oke, made from the root of the ti plant, did not imply a similar fondness for the natives. His allegiance to Tommy strengthened Mrs. Fortescue's resolve. The other seaman, E. J. Lord, was a handsome, curly-haired, strapping young man, an amateur fighter whose strength might be useful.

Both had stopped off at the Armed Services YMCA on the way in from the base and changed into civilian clothes. Now, crowding into Mrs. Fortescue's car, the four drove downtown to the Judiciary Building. It was early evening. The Palace grounds were comparatively deserted. They could now go through a dry run of the plan without anyone suspecting what they were up to, mark all entrances and exits of the Judiciary Building, note the paths by which the building could be approached. If, as they hoped, Kahahawai reported as usual next morning, they would be ready for him.

That night Mrs. Fortescue sent her daughter Helene to stay with Thalia on the pretext that she herself would be out late and did not want to leave Helene at home alone. Then, alone in the bungalow, Mrs. Fortescue sat at her desk, making the final preparations for the execution of her plan.

What was required, she had decided, was some sort of official-looking document—a kind of subpoena—to serve on Kahahawai, something which would command instant obedience on his part. A scuffle outside the Judiciary Building in broad daylight would be disastrous. She would have to devise something to minimize the danger of that happening.

Lacking a typewriter, she began to block-letter an imposing cover for such a document.

As a mast head for the cover, she took the authoritative title of the Territorial Police Commander, a Major Ross. As she concentrated on its printing she was unaware of the fact that she was misspelling a word. It appeared on the forged document as:

TERITORIAL POLICE
MAJOR ROSS COMMANDING

Would Kahahawai spot the error and know at once that it was a forgery? Unconscious of the spelling error, Mrs. Fortescue did not even consider the question.

Beneath the title she printed:

Summons To Appear

and followed it with Joe Kahahawai's name, unmindful of the fact that an actual document would have referred to him as Joseph.

It seemed to her then that the wording on the cover was insufficient. It lacked the fine print which usually appeared on such documents.

Lying on the chaise near her desk was a morning newspaper. She picked it up and looked through it, seizing on a phrase which appealed to her imagination. It read:

Life is a mysterious and exciting affair and anything can be a thrill if you know how to look for it, and what to do with opportunity when it comes.

She clipped it and pasted it to the lower half of the cover. She was sure that to Kahahawai's unpracticed eye, to his undoubtedly illiterate mind, it would look thoroughly official.

What possibly did not occur to her even for a moment, was that she had chosen a piece of cloying and naïvely romantic sentiment from a sob sister column in the style of Dorothy Dix or Beatrice Fairfax, and that this perhaps characterized her own feelings in the affair.

The daring adventure—illicit in every way—on which she was about to embark was as stimulating to her as the words in the clipping declared. It was "thrilling . . . mysterious . . . exciting." Staring at Kahahawai's "brutal, repulsive black face" as she called it, she was sure that she knew "what to do with opportunity when it comes."

It was perhaps even more than opportunity. It was a return to the "prank" period of her youth—the period when she had stopped traffic on Washington's streets in behalf of woman suffrage.

So pleased was she with the forged document, with its undeniable appearance of authenticity, that for the moment she could be forgiven for forgetting its purpose. Like the play, it began to look as if "the prank's the thing," rather than its unforeseeable consequences.

THIRTEEN

Mrs. Fortescue scarcely slept that night, but the knowledge that the plan was ready to be put into action, kept her tuned at high pitch the next day. She rose at dawn, alert and wide-awake. Her project was still perhaps more of a prank than a plan—a thrilling and exciting affair rather than a deadly serious attempt to outmatch native cunning by taking the law into her own hands, for when Tommy showed up early to inform his mother-in-law that the large Buick sedan which he had rented as part of the plan, was now parked in her driveway, she showed him the forged documents.

"See my grand warrant, Tommy!"

She was like a young girl in her delight with it. It was a work of art, as effective a lure as an angler's homemade fly.

They drank coffee together, chuckled over the clipping which she had pasted to the document. Even if Tommy noticed the misspelling, he was not bothered by it. The romantic quality of the clipping seemed so appropriate to their mission, an affirmation of its moral justice. They were disciples of St. George about to slay the evil dragon of opprobrium and native guile which had wrought so much havoc in their lives. To improve the document's apparent authenticity, Tommy detached a seal from a naval document, and pasted that too, to the cover. Only a purist would question its validity now.

The two seamen, Lord and Jones, had come in late the previous night after Mrs. Fortescue had gone to bed, and

were still asleep in the living room. While Tommy went
to wake them, Mrs. Fortescue prepared breakfast. Eggs
were cooking on the stove when they came into the kitchen,
but they wanted only coffee.

Jones started to check his pistol, but at Tommy's suggestion, it was decided that it might be unwise to go down
there armed. The gun was left lying on a kitchen shelf.
Tommy concealed his own gun behind the cushions of the
chaise in the living room . . .

Shortly after seven-thirty on that Friday morning, January 8, 1932, two cars started out of the driveway of the
Fortescue bungalow on Kolowalu Street and cruised slowly
down the quiet, colorfully landscaped, morning-scented
slopes of Manoa Valley toward the city.

In the official-looking Buick, Tommy, wearing gloves,
goggles and a fake moustache, sat behind the wheel. The
two seamen sat behind the "official" driver of the "official"
car. Mrs. Fortescue followed the Buick in her roadster.

Makai, toward the sea, a flag already flew from Honolulu's legendary and romantic Aloha Tower. Beyond the
reefs, interisland barges sailed across the glistening, tur-
quoise sea. Tourists had begun their early morning tours
of the Iolani Palace and its grounds. Busses and trolley cars
converged on the downtown area of the city. Children were
on their way to school. Beneath the surface calm of an
average end-of-the-week working day, the undercurrent of
racial hostility flowed unseen. The two cars melted into the
streams of morning traffic on King Street heading toward
their prearranged destinations.

As on the two previous mornings, Mrs. Fortescue parked
her car on South King Street where it intersects the Palace
grounds, perhaps fifty feet from the main entrance of the
Judiciary Building. The Buick was parked off to the right of
the building, near Honolulu's principal post office. It was
now a few minutes before eight o'clock.

The four held a hurried consultation. It was decided
that seaman Jones would be the bearer of the forged document and that he would take up a position in front of the
main entrance. Lord would serve as watchdog at the rear
of the building. Joe Kahahawai's picture was given to Lord
for final study. Tommy remained seated behind the wheel
of the Buick.

Officers of the Judiciary had begun to arrive. From her vantage point, Mrs. Fortescue spotted Mrs. Whitmore, the clerk of the court, entering the building. Even if Mrs. Whitmore had recognized her, it was unlikely that she would have connected her presence there that morning with the informative chat they'd had a few days earlier.

A minute or two later, Mrs. Fortescue saw the big Hawaiian. Accompanied by a young, much shorter man, he walked across the Palace grounds, past the closely huddled stands of the giant banyans, past the bandstand where the Royal Hawaiian Band would later in the day provide music for visitors. The two men passed within a few feet of Mrs. Fortescue's roadster. Kahahawai, towering over his companion, wore light-colored pants, a blue shirt and a brown cap. The two moved past the statue of King Kamehameha I, then entered the building.

Jones looked enquiringly toward Mrs. Fortescue. She nodded. Jones withdrew the forged document from a pocket and waited. Mrs. Fortescue's pulse quickened with anticipation. Her eyes fixed on the entrance to the building, she awaited the dramatic consummation of her plan, its masterful victory over laggardly and inhuman Island authority. In the Buick sedan, Tommy sat behind the wheel, waiting now for Kahahawai to reappear. Thus far, everything had gone exactly as planned. As in a sea trial, his vessel, so to speak, was now within firing distance of the target. It was the next step he was not too sure about, since it was one which could not have been rehearsed. Hitherto, in the execution of the preliminary tactics, his mother-in-law had been the leader. Soon it would be his turn to take over, to act on his own initiative.

Within the building, Kahahawai had reported to the court probation officer, his appearance duly recorded in his file. The young man who had accompanied him was a cousin, Edward Ulii. His presence was perhaps a safety measure, to ensure that Kahahawai had a witness to the fact that he had put in an appearance.

Within a few minutes both men reappeared on the steps of the Judiciary Building and started toward the Palace grounds. They had gone but a few paces when Jones moved up to Kahahawai and tapped him on the shoulder. The big Hawaiian turned to him.

"Are you Kahahawai? Major Ross wants to see you."

Jones showed him the document. The Major wanted to ask him a few questions about the events of the previous Saturday night, he said. Kahahawai had nothing to worry about, he added reassuringly. It was just a formality.

Kahahawai eyed Jones curiously. He stared at the document. The seal glinted in the morning sun. He did not know whether official documents all bore such seals, nor did he have time to examine the document, for Tommy had already drawn the car in close to where they stood.

"Get in," Jones said, and opened the rear door of the car. "Not him," he added when Kahahawai suggested that his cousin go along too. Jones got between the two Hawaiians, nudging Kahahawai into the car.

The order may not have seemed especially threatening to Kahahawai. It was not the first time he had been picked up. The white man had said there was nothing to worry about. Kahahawai knew Major Ross. He had served under him as a member of the National Guard. Had Kahahawai suspected that there was something wrong, he might have asked to examine the document more closely and might have noticed the amateurishly printed cover if not the misspelling. The sentimental clipping would undoubtedly have roused his suspicions. But apparently he did not feel that it was necessary to examine the document, or perhaps he was merely trusting the white man as his ancestors had trusted him.

Jones followed Kahahawai into the car and pulled the door shut. Tommy gunned the engine and the car sped away. Within moments Lord trotted up from the rear of the building and climbed into Mrs. Fortescue's roadster which moved out rapidly after the sedan.

Witnessing Jones's approach to Kahahawai, Mrs. Fortescue had glanced for a moment at the big Hawaiian's companion. He had stood there passively, listening to Jones. What she did not see was that the moment both cars had disappeared Edward Ulii turned and ran back into the Judiciary Building.

Even had she seen him, she was probably much too excited and engrossed with what lay ahead, to pay much attention to what his action might mean. All was going so smoothly—beautifully!

Not until he had been escorted into the living room of the bungalow on Kolowalu Street to find Tommy facing him, goggles and gloves off, fake moustache removed, Jones's .32 automatic pointed at him, did Kahahawai realize how completely he had been duped, how *lolo* he had been to trust the damned Haole.

There were three of them in the room with him now: Mrs. Fortescue, the powerful Lord—and Tommy, pale, quivering but determined, pointing the gun at him. Jones stood guard outside the room.

Mrs. Fortescue had, in her excitement, forgotten to close the front door. She now closed the living room door and blocked it with a chair, reluctant to leave this triumphant scene of confrontation even for the moment it would have taken her to instruct Jones to close the front door. She wanted to be eyewitness to each instant, to hear each guilty word, catch each incriminating flicker of an eye. This was the high point of the plan, the tremendous moment of confession.

She was to tell at a later time, and in her own way, of the almost unbearable tension of those minutes in her living room, of the grim, deadly and swiftly accelerating horror of Kahahawai's interrogation by Tommy as it moved closer and closer to the moment when it could no longer be borne, when it ended in a manner which could never have been consciously considered by her—and from which she would have shrunk aghast had anyone suggested that this had all along been her intention.

At mid-morning, scarcely two hours after Joe Kahahawai had stepped into the big Buick sedan in front of the Judiciary Building, the car was seen by a police officer as it came down from Manoa Valley at high speed and swung *waikiki*, toward Diamond Head, roaring off toward the Koko Head Road above the promontory. Rear blinds drawn as it sped past, the car tallied with a description which had been furnished him an hour earlier by headquarters, at the instance of Kahahawai's cousin, Edward Ulii. He had reported to the police that he believed his cousin had been kidnapped.

Within minutes, the police officer had overtaken the car and passed it, reporting by radio to headquarters that he had the car in sight. Pulling over to the side, he jumped out, drew his gun and gestured to the oncoming car to halt. His signal was ignored, the car swirling past so close that he was forced to leap aside. He fired twice after the racing vehicle, but it had already put a hundred yards between them. Soon it was out of sight on the curving road, heading uphill toward Maunaloa Bay and the jagged outcrop of Koko Head's shelving lava rock. He radioed for help and sped off in pursuit.

A car travelling the tortuous coastal roads of Oahu is, save for some reckless leap into the sea, bound to be overtaken; with help already on the way, his familiarity with the road enabling him to drive through the turns without reducing speed, the officer caught up with the car, forced it over to the shoulder where the ground fell sharply to the sea, and at gunpoint ordered the occupants out. There were three—two men and a woman. He knew two of them at once—Tommy and Mrs. Fortescue—for he was one of the officers who had testified in court to the effect that Thalia had said she remembered but one name, the name of "Bull." The other man was seaman Lord.

All three stood dutifully quiescent as the officer searched the men for weapons and accepted Mrs. Fortescue's haughty statement that she had no gun.

Now he searched the car. On the floor in back, clumsily wrapped in a damp sheet, was a form that could only be human. The officer was clearly shaken—already beginning to suspect whose form it was, for in the hasty wrapping, the bare, dark-skinned foot of a man had been left exposed. But he preferred to wait for help to arrive before making sure.

Mrs. Fortescue had seated herself on a shelf of rock to the side of the road. She sat there detached and aloof until a second police car arrived. And now the naked body of the man who lay on the floor of the car wrapped in a damp bed sheet was at once identified. There was the small, clean wound of a bullet above the heart. There were no blood stains on the sheet. In death, Joe Kahahawai lay as he must have slept, or floated perhaps on Oahu's warm sea.

Word was radioed back at once to headquarters. Soon, a convoy of city and county officials, the coroner, newspapermen and photographers arrived. An area left largely to the tourists was now besieged by hundreds of the curious.

An hour passed, during which time neither Mrs. Fortescue, nor Tommy, nor Lord would do much but make inconsequential small talk. They would answer no questions.

In the bright warmth of the morning, when the sun had reached its highest point, Mrs. Fortescue's magnificently conceived plan sank to its lowest. The three were bundled into a patrol wagon. They sat on either side of Joe Kahahawai's body which now lay in a wicker basket at their feet, shaken and jolted as they were, on the road back.

FOURTEEN

The disastrous news of the arrest of Mrs. Fortescue, Lieutenant Massie and the two seamen was communicated to Admiral Stirling much as the news of Thalia's rape had been.

(Jones, who had stayed behind to "clean up" when the others left with their fatal cargo, had been arrested at Thalia's home, where he had gone to await their return. In searching him, the police found the forged document as well as the .32 caliber clip from which the shot that killed Kahahawai had been fired.)

The Admiral had been about to leave his home to keep another exasperating appointment with Governor Judd and Hawaii's Attorney General, Harry R. Hewitt. There had been an announcement that the latter would personally conduct the prosecution in the retrial of the five defendants. It was the Admiral's hope in going to see these gentlemen again that this time he would be able to persuade them to reconsider their earlier decision and have the date of the retrial moved up.

How tiresome it all was, arguing with these stubborn Islanders! Yet, as the Admiral was himself to describe his feelings before the news of the arrest reached him, he would not allow the arduous purpose of his visit to Hawaiian officials to mar his pleasurable contemplation of Hawaii's magic. That very morning, in fact, the radiance of sea and sky and floral beauty had stirred in him "a delightful sense of the joy of living." It helped him forget (which it apparently did quite frequently) how effectively Hawaii

85

had been overrun by Asiatics and half-breeds. This refrain runs constantly through his memories of those difficult days. Hawaii's natural beauty also helped him forget "the very existence of sordid people whom a trusting Providence had permitted to exist on these heavenly Islands." He did not mention that it was the same trusting Providence which had permitted the plantation owners to recruit these "sordid people" as field hands.

"Admiral," he was told by his shore patrol commander when he re-entered his home to take an urgent call from the latter, "Kahahawai has been kidnapped by white men in a car in front of the courthouse. The police are hunting for them. I believe it was done by Massie!"

Not yet did either of them know that Kahahawai was dead. That was to come after the Admiral had left to keep his appointment with the Governor and the Attorney General. Nonetheless, en route to the Governor's palace, he could not help wondering, with a certain admiration, how so mild and self-effacing an officer as Lieutenant Massie had found the nerve to snatch the Hawaiian from under the very nose of the authorities. It was the sort of thing that in war time would have earned Tommy a Navy Cross.

It was Governor Judd who broke the news of Kahahawai's murder, and the arrest of his killers, to the Admiral. Deeply moved, pale with anger, the Governor made no bones about his feeling that what had happened was a direct result of the Admiral's encouraging a disregard for the laws of Hawaii.

The Admiral lightly dismissed the accusation. Any attempt to connect him with Kahahawai's death was palpably absurd . . . ludicrous. Not that he hadn't expected that something of the sort would happen. All five criminals should have been kept in prison, for their own safety if for no other reason.

If Kahahawai's death disturbed him, he showed little sign of it. It certainly did not cause him to forget the original purpose of his visit. Thoroughly composed, he blandly reminded the agitated Governor—a man who, as a descendant of missionaries put the welfare of Island people before everything else—that the "killing of one leaves four for the retrial. That's what I came to see you about."

The Governor was horrified by this sublime indifference to Kahahawai's murder.

"They have killed one of my people!" he exploded. "I'll bring those murderers to trial immediately!"

In a cold fury he informed the Admiral that he was not interested in the Ala Moana case.

Obviously, Governor Judd could not see the forest for the trees, Admiral Stirling mused regretfully. Clearly, there was nothing more left to discuss here. As for their friendship, it was at an end. He could only urge, as earnestly as he could, that the Governor would be wise to jail the four remaining rapists. It might save their lives.

Admiral Stirling, who had longed for some break that would give him reason to personally participate in the affair, now found that reason presented to him in a manner which made his intervention unquestioned. Clothed in the powerful authority of the Navy, he could march into the office of the District Attorney, dramatically and imperiously demand: "Take off those irons!"

Civil authorities had no right to handcuff any of his people! Navy men were sacrosanct! It was Lord who had been handcuffed. Luckily for the District Attorney, there were no handcuffs on the wrists of Lieutenant Massie or Mrs. Fortescue. Neither was Jones manacled. It is quite likely that the Admiral would have read the Articles of War to the Attorney General had either Tommy or Mrs. Fortescue been in irons.

His heart went out to this brave mother. With a gentle embrace, he assured her of his full support. To prevent the confinement of his own people in a filthy Hawaiian jail, he would have to act quickly, ride roughshod over Island authority.

Before the Admiral's dramatic appearance in the District Attorney's office, Mrs. Fortescue had been questioned by the public prosecutor. As though in some preposterous scene from *Alice in Wonderland*, the public prosecutor was the same man who less than a month ago had failed to convict the "lust-sodden beast" for whose death he was now committed to prosecuting the whites who had killed him. Did he perhaps feel culpable in what had happened because he had failed to win a verdict?

Yet the searching questions had to be asked.

"What is your name?"

"Grace Fortescue."

"You are the mother-in-law of Lieutenant Thomas Massie?"

"Yes."

"Mrs. Fortescue, what time did you leave your house this morning?"

"I don't know."

"Did you drive down in front of the Judiciary Building this morning?"

"I did."

"What time?"

"I don't know."

Days spent in the courtroom listening to Thalia's testimony had seemingly taught her that to express ignorance of time could be very useful. Without witnesses to contradict her, her lapses of memory could not be disputed.

"What was your purpose in driving down there?"

How plausible to be able to say: "It was the easiest place to park. I was going to the post office to mail some letters."

"How long did you sit in your car this morning?"

"I don't know. I didn't have a watch on."

"Did you see Joe Kahahawai come out?"

With superlative control—as glibly as a practiced and frequent defendant—she answered: "No!" and again "No!" when she was asked whether she had pointed Joe Kahahawai out to three men.

"When you parked there yesterday or the day before, what was your intention at that time?"

"I don't know."

"Mrs. Fortescue, did anyone sleep at your house last night other than yourself?"

"I don't know. I went to bed early."

"Was anyone at your house other than yourself this morning?"

Naturally, she didn't know, just as she did not know whether she or any enlisted men had drunk some coffee at her home that morning. Had she mailed her letters at the post office. No, because she had no envelopes. Yes, she had intended getting envelopes at the post office. Did she get them? No, she hadn't; nor did she know why she hadn't. In her negativeness, she had by now far outdistanced her daughter.

In her lack of observation she was at least as good. She hadn't seen the sedan car drive up in front of the Judiciary Building entrance. She hadn't seen Joe Kahahawai come out of the building.

Seaman Jones was brought into the room. His face was flushed. He was grinning rather foolishly. He had obviously had too much to drink.

"Have you seen that man before?"

"Surely. He took me to a baseball game."

"Did you see him today?"

"No."

"Where was your daughter last night?"

Even if the questions had been asked of her more in sorrow than in interrogatory anger, Mrs. Fortescue was perhaps beginning to wonder whether her strategy of negativeness was wearing thin. Ally though Griffith Wight had been all along, he was still the public prosecutor. Why had he asked her about Thalia? If Thalia had actually been privy to the plan, no one was ever going to learn it from her mother. Wight could very well be as much a victim of Island intrigue and deception and conspiracy as she was herself. Without realizing how conditioned to it all he had become, he might be springing a trap question on her.

It could easily be a trap, asking her where Thalia was last night.

She eyed him coolly. "I don't think I'll talk any more."

The Admiral, arriving toward the end of the interrogation, took her answer to mean that she could endure no more of this torment. He had seen a tear in her eye. He had also exchanged a smile with her. Both tear and smile were interpreted by him to mean that she was undefeated, that she would fight for justice to the end, just as he would himself—whatever it was that justice meant to him at that moment.

With the cloak of naval authority to support every step, he demanded now that there be no more questioning of Navy personnel or the relatives of said personnel. With the same power, he prohibited the removal of the prisoners to Oahu Prison.

Peremptorily, he demanded an order from the Court appointing Captain Wortman of the Submarine Base as a Court deputy into whose custody the prisoners must be released. The intimidated authorities raised no objection. The four were at once released, pending trial, and removed temporarily to the station ship *Alton* at Pearl Harbor. The ship was used by the Navy as a kind of floating bachelor officers' quarters.

For the time being the four were safe. The Navy was taking care of its own.

Bitterly, and with the utmost scorn, the Admiral observed the unseemly haste with which Island authorities went about their shameful business of bringing the four to trial. Yet they had dragged their heels so abominably in setting a date for the retrial of the natives who were far more responsible, to his mind, than the four white people, for Joe Kahahawai's death.

That Haoles and non-Haoles would at once take sides when news of Kahahawai's murder broke was anticipated by the authorities. That same afternoon, thousands gathered on the streets surrounding police headquarters. The police had already been alerted to such a contingency. They moved into the area wearing gas masks and carrying tear-gas bombs. The crowds were dispersed.

Tension gripped the city. Misinterpreting an order, an overzealous officer sounded the siren on Aloha Tower, a signal to the entire National Guard of Oahu to mobilize. Confused orders sent patrols and truckloads of uniformed men racing through the streets of Honolulu and out onto the country roads which led to the sugar and pineapple fields. A revolt of the field hands was feared. Armed guards patrolled the Iolani Palace grounds, stood guard at the Palace. The Island quivered with rumors of martial law, a Navy take-over, the momentary arrival of battle cruisers from the mainland. Oahu was in a state of siege and imminent panic.

By the following morning, a full report on both the assault on Thalia Massie and the death of Joe Kahahawai was being completed by Admiral Stirling for despatch to the Secretary of the Navy.

With the release of this report two days later, to the

mainland press, a sudden concern for the plight of white people in Hawaii exploded into immediate demands that something be done. Newspapers on the mainland, responding to the newsworthiness of a sensational racial situation in Honolulu—one which had never been seriously examined or exploited by the press—fed inflammatory headlines to a public which had listened too long to news of depression and unemployment. Trouble in Hawaii was almost a welcome respite, as well as an opportunity for scare headlines.

HAWAII CRATER OF RACIAL HATE!
MANY WHITE WOMEN ATTACKED
IN HAWAII!
BAYONETS RULE HAWAII AS RACES BOIL
IN KILLING!
MELTING POT PERIL!

Tabloids garnished the banquet of sensation with exotically spiced accounts of the frenzy of lust-mad natives, of insolent orientals indulging in orgies of criminal violence.

By the following Monday morning, barely three days after Joe Kahahawai's death, President Hoover had summoned his cabinet to discuss the "ugly situation in Hawaii." At the meeting, Admiral Stirling's report on the situation, colored by his subjective attitude to the non-Haole community, was submitted to the Cabinet. At once, an investigation of conditions in Honolulu was launched by Attorney General Mitchell. A Senate committee was formed to participate in the investigation. Among its members were such distinguished congressional leaders as Senator Vandenberg, Hiram Bingham and Jesse H. Metcalf of Rhode Island. They were joined by Secretary of the Interior, Ray Lyman Wilbur, and Secretary of War, Patrick J. Hurley.

Hawaii, America's Garden of the Pacific, was suddenly the infamous focal point of the mainland's glaring searchlight.

Governor Judd had responded to a frantic cable from the *New York Times* appealing for information on conditions in Honolulu with the reply: "You are advised conditions in Hawaii warrant no occasion for alarm. The law enforcement agencies have the situation fully in hand and are adequate to cope with all situations."

It was only to be expected that so cliché-ridden a reassurance would not be believed. If anything, its publication served to exacerbate mainland opinion. Why hadn't they known of these native excesses earlier? Who was responsible for the cover-up? The questions pointed directly at President Hoover's personal appointee, Governor Judd.

If there was native excess in Honolulu, one place where it was found was at the funeral of Joe Kahahawai. The excess was in the size of the crowd. Until then, only the funerals of Hawaiian royalty had drawn so many thousands.

There was a *lei* of bright orange and yellow ilima blossoms about his neck as he lay in his coffin. Ilima is the official bloom of Oahu. For hours, mourners, including some whites, filed slowly past his coffin.

Kahahawai's father, then divorced from the dead man's mother, addressed the mourners.

"During the time from my son's arrest until his death, he and I talked about the charges against him often, and he always maintained he was innocent. He took an oath in front of me saying: "Daddy, I swear before God that I never did anything wrong."

David Kama, the brother of a police officer who had been killed some years before while trying to arrest a sailor, then spoke to the gathering.

"Poor Kahahawai," he lamented, "those Haoles murdered you in cold blood. They did the same thing to my poor brother. These Haoles shoot and kill us Hawaiians. We don't shoot any Haoles, but they treat us like this. But never mind! The truth will come out!" He looked at the body. "You are not wrong. If you were they would not catch those murderers. Thank God they were caught!"

The mourners answered:

"Hilahila ole keia poe haole!"

Shame on those Haoles!

Far from feeling shame, the Haole Citizens' Organization for Good Government called a meeting on the roof garden of the Young Hotel, then a much more impressive hostelry than the fading commercial hotel it is today, and

Introducing the first and only complete hardcover collection of Agatha Christie's mysteries

Now you can enjoy the
greatest mysteries ever written
in a magnificent
Home Library Edition.

Discover Agatha Christie's world of mystery, adventure and intrigue

Agatha Christie's timeless tales of mystery and suspense offer something for every reader—mystery fan or not—young and old alike. And now, you can build a complete hardcover library of her world-famous mysteries by subscribing to The Agatha Christie Mystery Collection.

This exciting Collection is your passport to a world where mystery reigns supreme. Volume after volume, you and your family will enjoy mystery reading at its very best.

You'll meet Agatha Christie's world-famous detectives like Hercule Poirot, Jane Marple, and the likeable Tommy and Tuppence Beresford.

In your readings, you'll visit Egypt, Paris, England and other exciting destinations where murder is always on the itinerary. And wherever you travel, you'll become deeply involved in some of the most

ingenious and diabolical plots ever invented ... "cliff-hangers" that only Dame Agatha could create!

It all adds up to mystery reading that's so good ... it's almost criminal. And it's yours every month with The Agatha Christie Mystery Collection.

Solve the greatest mysteries of all time. The Collection contains all of Agatha Christie's classic works including *Murder on the Orient Express, Death on the Nile, And Then There Were None, The ABC Murders* and her ever-popular whodunit, *The Murder of Roger Ackroyd.*

Each handsome hardcover volume is Smythe sewn and printed on high quality acid-free paper so it can withstand even the most murderous treatment. Bound in Sussex-blue simulated leather with gold titling, The Agatha Christie Mystery Collection will make a tasteful addition to your living room, or den.

Ride the Orient Express for 10 days without obligation.
To introduce you to the Collection, we're inviting you to examine the classic mystery, *Murder on the Orient Express*, without risk or obligation. If you're not completely satisfied, just return it within 10 days and owe nothing.

However, if you're like the millions of other readers who love Agatha Christie's thrilling tales of mystery and suspense, keep *Murder on the Orient Express* and pay just $9.95 plus postage and handling.

You will then automatically receive future volumes once a month as they are published on a fully returnable, 10-day free-examination basis. No minimum purchase is required, and you may cancel your subscription at any time.

This unique collection is not sold in stores. It's available only through this special offer. So don't miss out, begin your subscription now. Just mail this card today.

☐ Yes! Please send me *Murder on the Orient Express* for a 10-day free-examination and enter my subscription to <u>The Agatha Christie Mystery Collection</u>. If I keep *Murder on the Orient Express*, I will pay just $9.95 plus postage and handling and receive one additional volume each month on a fully returnable 10-day free-examination basis. There is no minimum number of volumes to buy, and I may cancel my subscription at any time.   07013

☐ I prefer the deluxe edition bound in genuine leather for $24.95 per volume plus shipping and handling, with the same 10-day free-examination.   07054

Name_____

Address_____

City_____ State_____ Zip_____
                                                              AR1
                                        Send No Money...
                                        But Act Today!

BUSINESS REPLY CARD

FIRST CLASS   PERMIT NO. 2154   HICKSVILLE, N.Y.

Postage will be paid by addressee:

The Agatha Christie
Mystery Collection
Bantam Books
P.O. Box 956
Hicksville, N.Y. 11802

demanded of the more than one thousand influential Haoles who attended that they press at once for reform of the police department, and for at least a decade of military government which would impose laws that the natives would learn to obey.

Discreetly left unsaid, was the fact that four of their own kind had flouted the one universal law by the murder of Joe Kahahawai.

Death, said the League of Women Voters, whose representatives appeared before the Territorial Senate, should be the only penalty for rape!

It was quickly becoming clear that the Haoles of Honolulu, backed by the Navy and by mainland support, had chosen to take the offensive as the best means of defending their own. No white man, or woman, would ever be convicted of killing Kahahawai! That was to be the rallying cry of their offensive.

FIFTEEN

It was a theme, endlessly repeated, embellished with all the sinister horrors that fertile imaginations could cultivate, which now began to preoccupy both the Islands and the mainland—a theme of lust and terror in Paradise, of naked hatreds and savage revenge, of primitive desires and impotent justice.

The courage of the brave Haoles who manned the figurative barricades against the just as figurative lecherous hordes could not be adequately extolled. For it was now believed, because of the reiteration which encouraged that belief, that under the tranquil beauty of Hawaii lay a roaring inferno as terrifying as the "pit of eternal fire" which raged in the Hawaiian volcano of Kilauea.

The few voices which tried to appeal for calm appraisal of the situation, which said that the so-called terror did not exist, were lost in the clamor. Many a tourist who had dreamed of visiting the Islands, was now thankful that he had stayed home. The dream could be justifiably forgotten. Instead he could sit back and accept his abnegation amid the torrents of print which poured from the wire services, from the pens of feature writers and authors who now found in Honolulu rich new soil in which to plant a flourishing and fantastic crop. The novelist, John P. Marquand, wrote:

When a stranger on these shores strives to gain enlightenment concerning Honolulu's present condition, he soon becomes aware he is an off-islander. A clannish mystery, a courteous wall of silence and reserve lies between him and the oldtime residents. The descendants of the missionaries, however hospitable, keep him at a watchful distance when it comes to island talk. But when the stranger walks north of Nuuanu Avenue, that distance becomes even greater. There is a subtle mystery of the Orient about it. There is the smiling, indomitable courtesy of Japan. There is a veneer as concealing as lacquer . . .

This was Marquand at his most atmospheric and subliminally tainted best. Were the kamaaina elite, the old-time residents, being modest about their courage, or was that courteous wall of silence and reserve a construction out of their own sense of guilt? If they felt responsible for so-called conditions, it seems they were not going to confide in Marquand.

"It had to come!" rattled off Dorothy Mackaill, star of stage and screen, on her special-feature typewriter:

The beach boys—the kanakas or full-blooded Hawaiians have had many romances with rich American women who have gone to the Islands as tourists and been enthralled with its Eden-like fascination. The beach boys have been spoiled by so many American women paying attention to them. By contrast, they are extremely deferential when put in their place.

It is little short of disgraceful to see how some women lie on the beach at Waikiki in abbreviated bathing suits and permit the beach boys to rub them with cocoanut oil so that they will get a good tan.

Let me say right now that the mixed element now on the island of Oahu is living dynamite. There is an undercurrent of dislike which borders on hatred between the Hawaiians and the Japanese and other orientals. They never get along together. The Hawaiians and those who have married into white families are a very proud people. But the oriental element who spend so much time in the water or on the beach are sort of "half-baked." They seem to be a little off mentally. . . .

It would have been hard to find any connection between the lady's Hollywood-conditioned sociology and the five youths accused of raping Thalia Massie. They were not beach boys. Though of three different origins, they were friends who, on the night of the assault, had gone to a luau together, danced at Waikiki Park, driven home in the same car.

But it made ready reading for mainland fans of Miss

Mackaill. In her vast experience of Island conditions as seen from the *lanai* of the Royal Hawaiian Hotel, she would surely know that the oriental element in the Islands was half-baked and a little off mentally.

Just as provocative was the spirited and unequivocal defense of Mrs. Fortescue by Charmian London, the widow of Jack London.

What have other mothers done [after the unprovoked violation and unspeakable manhandling of a daughter], mothers of all bloods and stations? They have protected their daughters wherever possible, or, failing that, have avenged them according to breed and nature.

Get down to first principles. The protection of our own is a first principle more primitive, perforce, than the starting of wars, ancient and modern, at the drop of a hat . . .

Animal mothers fend for their young with tooth and nail and foot. Human mothers have ennobled themselves by heroic defence of offspring.

If there was some of her late husband's preoccupation with the instincts in what she wrote, with the anthropomorphic attributes of the animal world, there was little of his philosophy. But for the image of Mrs. Fortescue as human mother it was homage of the first order.

In a front page editorial, the Hearst newspaper chain blazoned its considered opinion that Hawaii was now ready for martial law!

The situation in Hawaii is deplorable!

It is becoming or has become an unsafe place for white women. Outside the cities or small towns the roads go through jungles, and in these remote places bands of degenerate natives or half-whites lie in wait for white women driving by. At least forty cases of such vicious outrages have occurred and nobody has been punished.

(The unsupported figure was taken from Admiral Stirling's report to the Secretary of the Navy. To say that it was exaggerated is to put it mildly.)

The whole island should be promptly put under martial law and the perpetrators of outrages on women tried by court martial and executed!

Until such drastic measures are taken, Hawaii is not a safe place for decent white women and not a very good place for self-respecting civilized men!

Not to be outdone by the Hearst press, the New York *Post* called for the impeachment of both Governor Judd and Ray Lyman Wilbur, the Secretary of the Interior.

Theodore Roosevelt would have ordered a battleship to bring the defendants home for fair trial. [I.e., the defendants in the murder of Joe Kahahawai, not the defendants in the rape case.] No one can read the account of the rape without knowing that the only possible degree of reparation lies in the death of the dogs who committed the crime!

The white rallying cry to take the offensive had now received a magnificent fillip. If the mainland was ready to impose martial law on the Islands so were they. It goes without saying, of course, that it would only be imposed on non-Haoles.

A first step toward such a law lay in an economic sanction which the Navy Department now disclosed. The annual maneuvers of the Fleet off Hawaii would proceed as planned, but Navy personnel would not be granted shore leave in Honolulu.

The decision resulted in an estimated loss of more than five million dollars in revenue to the city. It was a decision, as Admiral Stirling was to say, which was "richly deserved." In his mystique of white supremacy, this was no more than a foretaste of fitting punishment to come.

For obvious reasons, punishment was not given out as the official reason for the cancellation of leave. "The situation in Oahu was too tense to permit leave," announced Admiral William V. Pratt, Chief of Naval Operations; then, by way of *obiter dictum* which reinforced accelerating mainland sentiment, he declared that "American men will not stand for violation of their women under any circumstances. For this crime they have taken matters into their own hands repeatedly when they felt that the law had failed to do them justice."

It was really too bad, he felt, that the Navy was without authority to take over the trial of Mrs. Fortescue, Lieutenant Massie and the others. It was in fact, Mrs. Fortescue's participation in the killing of Joe Kahahawai which made such a solution impossible. She could not be tried separately. Nonetheless, he continued to hope that the case would never come to trial, but that if it did, a way could be found to have it transferred to the mainland.

Meanwhile, with Mrs. Fortescue's husband reportedly in a state of collapse after hearing the news of his wife's arrest, family friends and social leaders on the mainland surged to her side with cabled messages of sympathy and understanding. None doubted the rightness of what she had done and one of these, Mrs. Edward T. Stotesbury of Philadelphia made a specific promise of help which Mrs. Fortescue was later to remember with gratitude.

Yet, despite the overwhelming condemnation of Island authorities by the Navy, by the press, by Senators and Congressmen, by the millions who believed what they read in the papers, there were a few sane voices. The Hartford Courant editorialized:

The grief of the husband and the mother is easy to understand, but resort to the "unwritten law" cannot be justified.

The Nation, of modest but distinguished circulation stated categorically that—

the Hawaiian, Joseph Kahahawai was lynched. He was lynched not by a mob of moronic and passion-drunk irresponsibles out for a man hunt, but by a woman of refinement and breeding and by an officer of the United States Navy who is guilty incidentally not only of murder but of the rankest lack of discipline in ordering to his assistance two enlisted men in the commission of a major crime.

In Honolulu itself, the Star-Bulletin remained loyal to the Islands. Its editorial carried this succinct comment:

People who take the law into their own hands always make a mess of it. There is no justification in civilized society for lynch law methods or premeditated killing of any character.

The paper steadfastly refused to go along with the defenders of "honor slaying" and "the unwritten law."

That there was a certain amount of validity for mainland concern, though certainly not for some of the highly colored accounts of conditions in Honolulu, was borne out by the investigation which now got under way. The team of investigators was led by Seth W. Richardson, an Assistant Attorney General in the Justice Department.

Nonetheless, where Admiral Stirling in his report to the Secretary of the Navy, had referred to "the almost universal lack of sentiment against the enormity of the crime of rape," Richardson, in his findings stated: "I do not think it is just to claim that the Hawaiian people generally have any unusual tendency toward the commission of such crimes."

Admiral Pratt, Chief of Naval Operations, had made the observation that when "you let them [white tourist women] take too many familiarities with the boys on the beach, something is going to happen—and it did." The Richardson report stated:

We saw nothing in the tourist and beach conditions which excited our critical interest.

Admiral Stirling, in his report, had referred to forty cases of criminal assault in the first eleven months of the year. Richardson found that—

hospital records do not indicate any such conditions. In fact, it was conceded by Captain Pfeiffer of the Navy police that such report . . . could not be substantiated. Actually, only seven cases of sexual violence were reported to the emergency hospital in 1931.

Admiral Stirling had also given it as his opinion that "racial feelings are very strong." The Richardson investigation found that—

racial intolerance is at a minimum, and serious racial resentment seemed infrequent.

The Admiral was apparently referring to his own racial feeling.

It was in the Police Department and in the office of the Public Prosecutor that Richardson found serious signs of inefficiency and incompetence. While there were no

criminal rackets in Hawaii, no organized crime, no serious
flaw in the courts or in the operation of the jury system,
it was nevertheless true that the Public Prosecutor's office
was weak, that the police force was undisciplined, the
parole system loose, and that law enforcement generally
suffered from the relaxed, easy-going pattern of Island
culture.

Steps had been taken for a thorough reorganization of
the Police Department even before the Richardson investigators arrived in Honolulu. Admiral Stirling had been right
in demanding it. As for the Richardson report itself, its
comparatively mild criticism of Honolulu was published
too late to deflect mainland hostility. The Islands continued to be the prime target for punishment.

During the course of the Richardson investigation, Rus-
sell Owen, a *New York Times* reporter, was allowed by
the Navy to interview the defendants. It was the only interview so granted.

A pass signed by Admiral Stirling allowed Owen to board
the station ship *Alton* which lay in a mud flat a few hundred feet from Pearl Harbor's submarine base.

Mrs. Fortescue, "a tall, slim woman with blonde hair
and a narrow face which showed few traces of the harrowing experiences through which she had passed," invited him
into the wardroom and offered him coffee which was
brought by a steward. He wrote of this interview:

She is alert and smiling, and her eyes are quick with vivacity,
touched on this occasion with an expression of lively curiosity
and some wariness. But her manner was outwardly frank, and
there is no doubt that under less strained circumstances she
would be a woman of charm. She is a Southerner.

When he asked her how she felt she answered:

Mostly that I am glad it is all out in the open. Those days
when my daughter's name was suppressed, when it was not
known whether or not she had been the victim of an assault,
and when people looked curiously at us and wondered—those
were worse than these last few weeks. There is a great sense
of relief. She had a bruise on her cheek, you know, and people
asked questions about it, and it was awful. Now that the worst
is over I feel more at ease than I have in months.

Owen mentioned that she seemed to be bearing up well under the ordeal. She murmured:

My mind is at peace. I am satisfied, and I am not worrying.

Lieutenant Massie entered the wardroom at that point. He was in shirt-sleeves, seemingly relaxed, even able to comment with sardonic humor on some aspects of the case. He was somewhat pale, Owen observed, no doubt from the weeks of confinement on the ship.

Owen asked Mrs. Fortescue about her feelings when she was overtaken by the police on the road to Koko Head. She replied:

I think the strongest impression was being dumfounded that they wanted to know my name, that I could not keep it quiet. They had not mentioned my daughter's name in the first case, and I could not understand why they wanted mine or why it was made public.

Apparently Mrs. Fortescue considered herself not as one of the participants in the killing of Kahahawai, but as much a victim as her daughter, with as much right to anonymity as the victim of rape. With so powerful a defense mechanism at her disposal, one ceases to wonder why Owen found her "alert and smiling." She went on to say:

Now of course I realize that we bungled it dreadfully, although at the time I thought we were being careful. I can see now that we were not. I made the mistake of pulling the shade down in the car. I should not have done that. We did not know we were being fired at. We heard something but thought it was the car backfiring or a tire blowing.

Again she was dumfounded when they were stopped. This was of course a wry admission that even the best laid plans sometimes fail. But there was certainly no admission that there was anything criminal in those plans. It was just a pity that they had bungled it.

Now is seems she wanted to be sure he understood, for she said:

You must realize that we had been under a terrible strain; that we had all suffered as I did not know it was possible to suffer. There had been terrible slanders, and everything had been done to slander her [Thalia's] reputation.

If this were not justification enough there was always the loyal support of Admiral Stirling.

"A sentence which would send these people to a Hawaiian prison," he said now, "where they would live at hard labor with Orientals and other dark-skinned criminals was horrible even to contemplate. It must not happen!"

Like Admiral Pratt and members of Congress, he demanded a change of venue to a mainland court. Representative Virgil Chapman of Kentucky warned his fellow congressmen that it would be unsafe to turn Lieutenant Massie over to a native jury. As for the defendants in the Ala Moana case, he said, "There is not a jury in the United States that would have failed to convict the native who was killed."

The General Assembly of Kentucky, Tommy's home state, voted a resolution demanding that every arm of the government be called into use to ensure immediate release of the four defendants and that President Hoover declare martial law in Honolulu until such time as Hawaii can be made safe for women!

If there was no serious racial resentment in Honolulu, as the Seth Richardson investigation found, there was enough and to spare on the mainland to save Mrs. Fortescue and Tommy from too much anxiety about their eventual fate.

Thalia, whether or not she was aware of all the efforts that were being made to achieve the release of the defendants, remained safely in seclusion in her Manoa Valley home. The tide of Haole anger, of mainland furore, had turned from concern with her case to that of the others. Her own ordeal had, for now, become a mildly remembered prelude to the thunderous and compelling music which had brought her mother and her husband to the center of the stage.

SIXTEEN

With brushfire suddenness, the news raced through Honolulu that the case against Mrs. Fortescue, Tommy and the two seamen, Lord and Jones, was going to be dropped!

Just as suddenly came the disappointing report that it wasn't altogether true, although it had come very close to being so.

In their first report to Judge Albert M. Cristy, it was learned now that the Grand Jury's vote was twelve to nine for no true bill. Instead of accepting this report, Judge Cristy released one of the jurors—a newly appointed police commissioner who was then participating in the reform of Honolulu's Police Department—and ordered a new vote taken by the remaining members. The result was still against the indictment of the four defendants by a vote of eleven to nine.

Admiral Stirling was to say later that had the judge accepted the first vote there would have been no trial and the defendants would have been freed. However, Judge Cristy, whose sense of justice would not allow him to tolerate the Grand Jury's disregard of the facts in the case, now charged the Grand Jury to consider an indictment for second-degree murder. No sooner did news of the Judge's intervention reach the mainland than Senator Kenneth McKellar of Tennessee reacted angrily to this affront to the white race and demanded Judge Cristy's impeachment.

Nothing came of the demand, and a true bill on a charge of second-degree murder was returned, albeit reluctantly, by the preponderantly white panel.

Now that all his efforts to prevent the trial had failed,

Admiral Stirling, recalling the failure of the prosecution
to convict in the Ala Moana case, a failure which in that
instance he believed to be purely the result of legal incompetence, now wondered whether the prosecution had
learned too well from that experience. They might even
be competent enough to win!

Executing a one-hundred-and-eighty-degree turn in his
approach to the problem, he now urged the defendants to
look to the mainland for the best legal talent they could
find to defend them. Superb helmsman that he was he had
swung his ship of justice about to confront the enemy from
the opposite direction.

The offer of help which Mrs. Fortescue had received
from Mrs. Edward T. Stotesbury of Philadelphia now made
it possible to appeal to a man whose wisdom, integrity and
inspired eloquence in the defense of people be believed
to be unjustly arraigned, had earned him that very year,
a graphic and moving description as "Attorney for the
damned." He was the Man from Kinsman—Clarence
Darrow.

The $25,000 retainer offered to Darrow by Mrs. Stotes-
bury was tempting. The stock market crash had wiped out
the savings he had managed to accumulate in half a century of active court life. Yet, as he himself said, he was
not certain that he could bear the daily routine, "beginning
in court early each day, watching and catching all that
goes on in a trial . . ." He doubted whether his mind
would "click with its oldtime vigor."

But the case interested him. Primarily, he saw it, not
as an outgrowth of racial conflict, but as a question of
causes and motives. It was a study in psychology, and this
had always intrigued him.

The more he read about the case, the stranger and more
puzzling it became. He began to feel that he wanted to
take it. He was frank enough to admit to friends and relatives of the defendants that he had misgivings about his
ability to conduct the defense with all the alertness and
ability that it required. But they decided to take a chance.

Clarence Darrow was almost seventy-five years old. His
entire life as a lawyer had been devoted to defense. He

had never prosecuted anyone. Certainly this was another case for his defensive genius. But there was a factor here which perhaps did not occur to him immediately. In the famous trial of Leopold and Loeb, eight years before, he had led the defense in an atmosphere in which both public and press had been almost solidly against the defendants. Defense of the underdog had always been the leitmotiv of his courtroom career. It was his life style. "I speak for the poor, for the weak, for the weary," he had said a quarter of a century earlier when defending William "Big Bill" Haywood, who was being tried in the bombing assassination of Frank Steunenberg, former Governor of Idaho, "for that long line of men who, in darkness and despair, have borne the labors of the human race."

This was still his pattern, the spine of his personality. In reading the accounts of Kahahawai's death, he, like the millions of others who had read the same accounts—or, as he said rather surprisingly, "like most persons with imagination"—wanted these people to win.

But in coming to the decision to take the case, he had overlooked the fact that whereas public sentiment had been against the defendants in the Leopold and Loeb case, both public and press were almost solidly for these defendants. This new situation ran counter to the atmosphere in which he had conducted so many of his cases. Like Phocion, the Athenian disciple of Plato, he might characteristically have asked himself when applauded by the crowd, what he had done amiss. But it seems that he had forgotten this pivotal hinge in his personality: that public support might blunt the thrust of his defense.

Though Darrow had shut down his law practice four years earlier, he went about the business of preparing himself for trial with all the intensive, searching energy of earlier days. From a colleague, William (Wild Bill) Donovan, who in World War II was to head the Office of Strategic Services—the cloak and dagger branch of the military—he learned that Donovan's law partner, George S. Leisure, had once tried a case in Hawaii. He at once called Leisure and invited him to lunch. He wanted all the information Leisure could give him on Hawaiian law. Leisure, a much younger man, and a great admirer of Darrow, told him all that he knew.

His experience in the Islands, plus the fact that he'd had some additional experience as a District Attorney, persuaded Darrow that Leisure would be of great help in the case. He invited him to join in the defense. Leisure, delighted with this rare and unexpected privilege of working with the man he considered to be the finest criminal lawyer of his time, accepted promptly and gratefully.

"In the fate of the defendants," Darrow had written in the story of his life, "there is scarcely anything more important than the setting and surrounding of the drama."

Thus, since Hawaii and its people were entirely new to him, he intended making it a matter of first consideration. That he had much to learn in the short space of the week the court had granted him for preparation did not seem to him to be as difficult as it did to others.

Very soon after his arrival in Honolulu, Darrow became aware of native hostility and resentment, a brooding anger over the death of Kahahawai. He and his wife, together with the Leisures, had taken rooms at the downtown Young Hotel, declining the Royal Hawaiian Hotel's offer of free accommodation. Darrow wanted no enchanted surroundings during his stay. He wanted to observe and understand.

Between periods devoted to a study of the facts in both cases, and to poring over the statements of witnesses and persons involved which had been prepared for him by Montgomery Winn, one of the attorneys engaged by the defendants before it was known whether Darrow would take their case, he sallied forth on his observation of the Island and its people.

Soon, perhaps in a prompt effort to "modify" the settings and surroundings, he issued a statement which read, in part:

. . . most opinions regarding conditions in Hawaii which have been circulated on the mainland are just so much poppycock. There is no racial problem whatsoever. People are just as safe in Hawaii as in any mainland community. Whatever feeling exists may be class feeling; but it is not racial feeling. I am entirely satisfied that Hawaii should be left alone.

He had not come, he wanted the citizens of Honolulu

to know, as a defender of white supremacy. He would not conduct the trial on the basis of race. Race prejudice was as abhorrent to him as were the fanatics who practiced it.

If his supply of oil for the troubled waters was inadequate, it was at least a good beginning. He could now get down to the practical business of gathering more facts, more evidence, interviewing the defendants, Navy personnel, local officials as well as the man in the street, taking no notes, but relying on his retentive memory to come to his aid when he needed it.

In studying the testimony of the first trial, in meeting Tommy and Thalia, he became more and more prejudiced in their favor. Thalia, whom he described as a "clever, unassuming, attractive young woman," had positively identified four of the defendants in the rape case. This he believed to be true, just as he believed that, except for a single digit, she had correctly identified the license number of the Ida car.

As for the native defendants themselves, he took for truth a description of them as "gangsters" in the New York or Chicago style.

Although he had said that he intended making the Island and its people a matter of first consideration, he had apparently neglected to consult any of the literature or the professionally trained observers in the community who might have been able to correct some of his impressions.

He also took for truth what was largely the prosecution's position, that Thalia had left the Ala Wai Inn on the night of the assault to get some fresh air. Her departure had caused no special concern, he assumed, because it was the sort of thing she had done before. That is to say, when she no longer cared for the gaiety, she had gone home alone.

Thus it seems that despite his own avowed and uncompromising attitude to racial prejudice, he had already, without perhaps realizing it, accepted the white version of the affair.

It was in this frame of mind, then, that Darrow, grizzled and slightly bowed, his magnificently commanding and craggy face etched with the patina of age, went to trial.

SEVENTEEN

The Massie Case, as it would henceforth be known and passionately discussed, was far more than a murder trial. The case had made the Territory a battleground for the right to self-government against mainland domination, against the unwritten law of white supremacy—a law which now included among its articles of faith, the honor of American womanhood. The case had become a question, not of factual guilt, but of clear and present danger to white morality. The upholders of this morality could quote Darrow himself who had said: "There should be no trials, no lawyers, no judges to pass upon moral guilt."

No one, least of all the members of Hawaii's government, including Governor Judd, doubted that on the outcome of the trial would depend whether or not Hawaii would be stripped of its territorial powers, its hopes of Statehood gone, and the Islands placed under military rule.

The threat of the latter pointed like a battleship's big guns at the "dingy little tropical courtroom," as a regionally oriented reporter called it, where, on April 4, 1932, the trial began.

So large was the assembly of reporters assigned to cover the trial for press, periodicals and radio across the nation and around the world, that an entire adjoining courtroom had to be converted into a press room to accommodate them.

In the public section of the courtroom—filled to capacity as it would be each day—sat the divorced parents of Joseph Kahahawai. They would be present at every session of the trial along with social leaders of the Haole community, many of them women. Haoles and non-Haoles alike were to spend whole nights waiting outside the Judiciary Building each day, reluctant to forego a single episode in the drama of justice versus morality.

Every day during the course of the trial, a contingent of Navy representatives, headed by Admiral Stirling, appeared in the courtroom. The Admiral, though wearing civilian clothes, provided the Damoclean menace. His presence did not intimidate the new public prosecutor, John C. Kelley, any more than did the presence of Clarence Darrow. Kelley, not yet forty, a big, bulky Irishman with the passion and aggressive self-assurance of his race in his voice, was later to give violent expression to his opinion of the Navy.

The defendants arrived early on the opening day of the trial, delivered to the court by Navy transportation. The whine of their sirens as they swung into the Iolani Palace grounds and pulled up before the Judiciary Building reached the Governor's office in the Palace on the *mauka* side of the grounds. Its note ricocheted through the offices of the Territorial legislators, scattered the birds in the thick, dark tangle of the banyans.

Of Mrs. Fortescue, Darrow has said that he found her to be "an attractive woman of intelligence and force of character." His opinion of Tommy was that he was "a kindly, sympathetic, human young man, generally liked by all who came in contact with him. I have seldom had a client for whom I formed a stronger affection." Of the two seamen, Lord and Jones, he said that they were "strong, fearless and loyal, and like all sailors, devoted to Lieutenant Massie."

That this description of Lord and Jones was mere romantic generalization was soon to be discovered, when he turned to the public prosecutor in the course of the trial and asked the name of one of the seamen.

Kelley eyed him in surprise: "Don't you know?"

"Yes—but it popped my mind," said Darrow.

Four months earlier, Mrs. Fortescue had spent many days in this same building, if not the same courtroom, a silent but determined ally of the prosecution. Now, just as silent, as aloof and patrician as ever, she was a defendant. The prosecutor was her enemy. She was convinced that what she had done was not illegal, that in her scheme to obtain a confession from Kahahawai, she had broken no law. In her own words, "We were endeavoring to aid the law."

Whether or not her convictions were shared by Tommy, his manner in the courtroom expressed anxiety. He sat rigidly self-controlled, pale, solemn, his mouth tight, overcompensating for his concern.

It is doubtful whether at that moment he remembered that four years before both he and Thalia had faced a judge in a tiny Long Island courtroom, charged with the kidnapping of an infant. It was nothing serious really, just one of Thalia's pranks. Strangely enough, he now faced the bench in a Hawaiian courtroom, codefendant with an older and much more skillful a player of pranks. Her skill had ended in disaster.

Why hadn't he opposed the plan? Was it some mistaken sense of Southern chivalry which would have made it ungracious to reject it? The matriarchal persuasiveness of this magnificently confident Southern beauty had blinded him to all the dangers, landed him in the gravest crisis of his life.

Lord and Jones, wearing civilian clothes, as was Tommy, did not seem to be aware of the gravity. The Navy always took care of their own. It would take care of them now. Navy personnel had raised a $7,000 defense fund for them. They were heroes. Jones had spent a lot of time during his stay on the *Alton* compiling a scrap book. His face was known to millions.

The first four days of the trial were devoted to the selection of a jury. Questioning of prospective jurors was undertaken for the prosecution by Kelley's associate, Barry Ulrich, a man of delicate physique and icy personality, who would no more allow Darrow's predilection for causes and motives to interfere with the due process of law than he would entertain the acceptance of any juror who might be overawed by Darrow's reputation.

He had put the question to one prospect: "I suppose you know Mr. Darrow as you do Abraham Lincoln or President Hoover or any other great man?"

The juror said that he did not, whereupon Ulrich was prepared to accept him. Darrow rose to question the man. In a few brief thrusts he drew the admission from the man, a Hawaiian, that his education had never gone beyond the fourth grade. He also admitted to having expressed an opinion that the defendants should be shot. He was excused.

As the tedious business of jury selection proceeded, Darrow's fear that his mind might not click with its old-time vigor, seemed to be dispelled. He was watching and catching all that goes on in a trial. Though his body might not be as quick as those of his adversaries, his mind leapt at once into play when a prosecution maneuver threatened his own position.

Already in the questioning of prospective jurors there had arisen the controversial issue of whether or not the Ala Moana trial could be introduced by the defense. The prosecution wanted it kept out of the case. Kelley, taking over the questioning of one prospective juror, reminded him that the guilt or innocence of Kahahawai in the Ala Moana trial had nothing to do with the present case. He wanted to be sure the juror understood that.

Before the juror could answer, Darrow was at once objecting: "It might have something to do with it," he said. "I can imagine a number of situations where it would."

His voice was slower, deeper, hoarser than in earlier years. But it made its points with the same vibrant and telling effect.

Judge Charles S. Davis, a New Englander and a Harvard graduate who had lived most of his life in Hawaii, was asked by Kelley to instruct the jury there and then that the guilt or innocence of the murdered man in the Ala Moana case was immaterial.

It was the Judge's opinion that the case should not be introduced, unless of course reference was made to it in the testimony at which time he might find it necessary to instruct anew. For Darrow this was to be a vital aspect of his defense strategy.

The jury as finally chosen was composed of six white men and six non-Haoles, two of whom were Chinese, one Hawaiian-Chinese, two Hawaiian-American, the remaining non-Haole containing within his own heritage the encapsulated record of Hawaii's history, for in his antecedents there were Hawaiian, Tahitian, French, Scotch and Irish.

Would it hurt his case, Darrow was asked, since, because of their ineligibility, there were no women on the jury?

Darrow's answer was blunt and characteristic.

"Women are more cruel as judges of their own kind than men!"

"Gentlemen of the jury, these defendants are charged with the crime of murder in the second degree!"

It was John C. Kelley who thus opened the case for the prosecution before going on to read the official indictment. The suggestion of brogue in his voice intensified the gravity of the indictment, the power and dignity of the law, the archaically sonorous yet damning language by which, "The Grand Jury of the First Judicial Court of the Territory of Hawaii do present that Grace Fortescue, Thomas H. Massie, Edward J. Lord and Albert O. Jones, in the city and county of Honolulu, in the territory of Hawaii, and within the jurisdiction of this honorable court, on the eighth day of January, 1932, through force of arms—to wit, a certain pistol loaded with gunpowder and a bullet, a more particular description of which is to the grand jury unknown, held in the hands of them . . . did unlawfully, feloniously and with malice aforethought and without authority and without justification or extenuation by law, did kill and murder Joseph Kahahawai Junior, a human being, and did then and thereby commit the crime of murder in the second degree contrary to the form of the statute in such cases provided."

Kelley wore tropical whites, symbolically perhaps, in marked contrast to Darrow in his customary dark, loosely fitted suit, carelessly knotted tie, the old-fashioned watch chain looped across his vest.

Kelley's opening statement to the jury was made with the supreme confidence of a man who had so familiarized himself with every aspect of the case that he had only to make the statement for it to be crystal clear to everyone that the accused were guilty. If his associate, Barry Ulrich, winced at the florid, baldly simplistic manner of his speech, it did not change the honesty and directness of his attack:

". . . Joseph Kahahawai entered the building, reported to Mr. Dickson [the probation officer], and then rejoined his cousin. When they arrived almost at the statue of Kamehameha, under the shadow of its outstretched hand, the finger of doom pointed at one of the members of that king's people. That finger was pointed by Mrs. Fortescue. In the vernacular, she put Joseph Kahahawai on the spot!"

It was irresistible that he implement the accusation by pointing a finger at Mrs. Fortescue. If, with his flair for the melodramatic, he expected her to cringe, he was disappointed.

Necessary though it was for the prosecution to reconstruct the crime in all its incriminating detail, this did not seem, however, to be having the desired effect. It was as if those who listened both in the courtroom and on the mainland—reading the cabled reports in the press, or listening to the testimony as it was broadcast—were prepared to concede that this was what had happened, that it was all as true as the prosecution stated. They wanted it to be over so that the Court might come to the heart of the matter. In the minds of the vast majority, the decision had already been made that what the defendants had done was completely justified. They had resorted to the unwritten law which, by its very nature, exonerated them. And, like Admiral Stirling, they wanted the Court to decide "that these defendants were not criminals, but merely human beings fighting for justice against an inhuman system!" For the Admiral had already made up his mind that although "a life had been taken . . . was it a life worth saving?"

Kelley was fully aware of white impatience, of the squirming annoyance with his recital of facts, but he had no intention of bowing to this implicit pressure to get it over with. By God! They would have to sit and listen to it all!

"We will show you and reconstruct for you, that after Kahahawai was taken into that house, he was shot! He was taken into the bathroom where he bled to death! His clothes were torn from his body and thrown into the bathtub to remove the blood. His trunks were split and two buttons ripped off and rolled under the bathtub!"

He would spare them no single detail of what they had done. The Islands and the mainland, and the defendants, and Clarence Darrow, would have to listen to every word!

"We will show they took the sheets from the double bed and wrapped the body in it, binding it with this rope . . ."

(He held up the length of rope with an identifying purple thread which meant that it was Navy property.)

". . . then took the body away in the sedan . . . We will show that there was no struggle in the house that might allow these defendants to claim self-defense as an extenuation for killing Kahahawai. And in that connection we will show that Kahahawai was a strong athlete, capable of putting up a good fight, and that there is no evidence of such a fight in the house.

"When we prove these matters to your satisfaction, we will ask you to bring in a verdict of guilty against each and every one of these defendants!"

But long before he had ended his opening statement, it was clear to many, as it certainly was to Darrow, that what the prosecution intended to show might not necessarily prove the defendants' guilt, since the prosecution's case was built wholly on circumstantial evidence. Nothing was really known of what had actually occurred in the Manoa Valley bungalow. It was not known who had held the gun or fired the shot. The gun had in fact, never been found. The prosecution knew only of the events leading to Kahahawai's abduction, and of the capture of three of the defendants by the police, when Kahahawai's body was discovered in their car.

Circumstantial evidence could of course be just as convincing as direct evidence. For Darrow to have based his strategy on the lack of the latter would have been absurd. Nonetheless there was tremendous curiosity as to what he would say. He chose to say nothing.

"If it please your Honor, the defense will reserve its opening statement."

At once speculation arose as to the strategy he had in mind, or whether he had any strategy at all. By evening however, speculation ceased, when it was learned that Darrow had already sent to the mainland for alienists, a step which the prosecution quickly countered by applying for funds to secure expert psychiatric witnesses of their own.

If Darrow saw the plight of the defendants as a study

in psychology, if it was into causes and motives that he was going to delve, it was a strategy in which, as everyone knew, he excelled.

Was Thalia to be a participant in that strategy? No one knew. Like Tommy, at the Ala Moana trial, she was a notable absentee at the proceedings.

EIGHTEEN

If, as seemed certain now, Darrow intended to make the
case a study in psychology, it became just as certain to
Kelley that it could lead in only one direction: to a plea
of insanity for whichever one of the defendants had fired
the gun. For the time being, however, Kelley would hold
off making any allusion to this possibility. There were
witnesses for the prosecution to be examined and cross-
examined, all unlikely candidates for psychological study.
They were simply eyewitnesses to facts. His examination
of them would be as direct and unsubtle as his opening
statement.

"As you approached this building, did you see anyone?"

He asked the question of his first witness, Edward Ulii,
the slightly built cousin of Joe Kahahawai who had accompanied the latter to the Judiciary Building that Friday
morning.

"Yes, a woman in a car on the ewa side of the building.
She was looking at Joe and I."

"Did you see anyone else?"

"Yes, a man on the ewa side of the entrance."

"Then what happened?"

"When Joe was finished, we walked out. The man was
still there yet. We walked toward King Street."

"And what happened?"

"I turned my head and saw the same woman in the
roadster car pointing at Joe and I. We stopped at King
Street to let the cars go by, and the man that was standing

by the entrance walked up to me and Joe and said that 'Major Ross wants to see you, Joe.'"

"Did you see any cars?"

"Yes—a car coming from the post office way into King Street. It stopped where we were. A man in the car opened the back door. A man came up to Joe and told Joe to get into the car. He showed him a paper."

"What kind of a paper?"

"White paper with a seal."

"Did Joe get in?"

"Yes."

"Then what did he do?"

"He said, 'Cousin, get into the car.' I put my foot on the running board. The man closed the door. He said, 'Wait here . . . we'll be back soon.' I watched the car drive away."

Ulii identified Jones as the man who had shown Kahahawai the forged document, then pointed to Lieutenant Massie as the driver of the car. He looked at Mrs. Fortescue, and said that she was the woman he had seen seated in the other car.

Ulii had been singularly observant that morning, it seemed. From his testimony one might have gathered that he was alert to danger from the outset, as though every person or waiting car that he saw was suspect.

Darrow could no doubt have found a way to discredit some of his remarkably perceptive testimony had there been anything to gain by it, but the indisputable fact in the testimony was that Kahahawai had been lured into the car. As a consequence, his cross-examination of Ulii was perfunctory, as it would be with many of the prosecution's witnesses.

Rarely had he tried a case where there was less real conflict in the evidence as it was presented.

"There was really nothing to be denied," he said later.

The law, he knew only too well, was on the side of the prosecution. His task was to convince the jury that "life, and all the human qualities that preserve it, was with us."

The irrefutable evidence continued to pile up against his clients. William Dickson, probation officer for the five defendants in the Ala Moana case, told of Mrs. Fortescue's visit to the court, when she had asked him about a rumor that two of the defendants had contrived their own arrest on the Island of Hilo. Not knowing that her questioning was a part of her scheme, he had informed her that the rumor was false, that the boys were reporting regularly at specific times of the day.

Again there was nothing to be denied by Darrow, nor was there anything subsequently when, in grim succession, police officers told of halting the car and finding the dead man's body, of identifying him and discovering the bullet hole, of searching the car and finding a blood-stained towel which bore the blue initials USN.

There was a momentary glimpse into the real feelings of Mrs. Fortescue and Tommy when a radio patrol officer was called as a witness.

He had arrived on the Koko Head Road soon after the car had been halted. He had stood there guarding the defendants as the body of Kahahawai was being identified.

Unexpectedly, Mrs. Fortescue turned to him and asked, "Haven't we met before?"

It was a strangely irrelevant question at such a moment. He told her that he didn't think they had ever met.

"Didn't you come down on the SS 'Maui' with me?" she persisted.

No, he said, he had not.

"It was someone who resembled you," she said then.

It was all as though in that moment of dreadful fear—fear that she would never admit—a moment of guilty terror not unlike that of Lady Macbeth when there came a knocking at the door, she had sought, in that pitifully inept attempt at social chit-chat, someone who would save her.

The radio officer, turning away from her in a kind of uncomfortable awareness of what she was attempting, placed himself firmly on the other side. "Good work, kid," he said to the officer who had halted the car.

But it was Tommy who answered him.

"Are you speaking to me?"

The radio officer made no comment. As though in some wry, perverse follow-up to the inglorious failure of the plan, Tommy shook hands with himself.

"Thank you very much," he said.

It was the ironic gesture of the loser in the ring, mocking

the gesture to the crowd of the winner, asking for at least some share of sympathy because he had made the other's triumph possible.

The prosecution was to recall this incident later.

The unassailable recital of evidence went on.

A medical officer testified that the cause of death was hemorrhage from a bullet wound penetrating the left pulmonary artery. The bullet was marked as an exhibit.

A police detective testified to searching the bungalow on the afternoon of the murder. He found Mrs. Fortescue's purse containing Kahahawai's picture. In a closet filled with women's clothes he found the torn shirt. He found Tommy's automatic under a cushion of the chaise. The cap which Kahahawai had worn that day was found in the living room.

A gas station attendant told of renting the Buick sedan to a friend of Lieutenant Massie's.

Said another police officer that he had found two pearl buttons in the bathroom which matched those on Kahahawai's trunks.

A noise like a shot was heard coming from the Fortescue bungalow by a neighbor, one of the rare Manoa Valley residents who was impartial.

A sporting goods salesman testified that he had sold Jones a .32 caliber Colt automatic and a clip of cartridges on December 17. He had also sold Mrs. Fortescue a .32 caliber Iver Johnson revolver and fifty cartridges, two days earlier. The purchase of the gun by Mrs. Fortescue did not necessarily prove premeditation. After all, Admiral Stirling had approved of the fact that Navy wives had begun to carry pistols for their own protection.

Inspector of Detectives John McIntosh, the same Inspector who had taken a statement from Thalia on the night of the rape, now testified to the arrest of the seaman Jones. He had found him in the living room of Thalia's home. There was a glass of liquor in his hand. He was drunk. Thalia was present.

In his testimony there were all the ingredients of some madly Gothic game of musical chairs. The man who had as good as admitted driving the Ida car around the old quarantine grounds in an abortive frame-up attempt, was now compelled to pull the chair out from under himself, as it were, and race for a chair on the other side.

The last witness to be called by the prosecution was the mother of Joe Kahahawai, Esther Anito. With her presence on the stand, whatever sympathy the jury may have already felt for the defendants might well evaporate. For here was the true *mater dolorosa*, whose son had been crucified by the Haoles.

This appeal to the emotions was obviously not to Darrow's liking. He wanted to concede that the clothing which Mrs. Anito was about to identify belonged to her son. But Kelley would have none of it. He wanted every last stitch shown both to the jury and the witness, just as he had insisted on the recital of every last shred of evidence by his witnesses.

Yes . . . that was his shirt . . . his socks . . . his dungarees. Questions were interpreted into Hawaiian for her, but she answered in halting English.

"His clothes were all washed . . . and I had sewed the buttons on."

"Was Joe in good health that morning when he left you?"

"Yes."

"When did you see him again?"

She was a big woman. Size had once been a valued distinction among Hawaiian women. Now she seemed pathetically overburdened by the flesh.

"At the undertaker's, on Saturday."

"That was the body of your son Joseph?"

"Yes."

It was not pleasant to see her and hear her. Justifying the crime could not change the bereavement.

It was now Darrow's opportunity to lend himself to that justification. He was going to bring home to people the "inherent rightness" in what they had done.

The Islands, the Navy, Washington and the nation wondered how he would go about it.

NINETEEN

Although the trial had occupied the front pages of Island and mainland press for more than a week, it was now sharing much of the space with the kidnapping of the Lindbergh baby. A typical day's headlines had brought Tommy into strange juxtaposition with Colonel Charles A. Lindbergh.

MASSIE TAKES STAND

LINDBERGH CONTINUES HUNT FOR HIS CHILD

If there had once been any physical resemblance between the two men there was very little now, either in appearance, or in the particular torment which each in his own way must have felt. Yet in the public mind there was perhaps a parallel, a kind of displacement of feeling from the ordeal of a father to the ordeal of a husband.

Rising with an abrupt movement when his name was called, Tommy walked to the stand. His voice was unnaturally loud when he took the oath. It was as if in his anxiety he could control neither his reactions nor the volume of his voice. He had lost weight. Out of uniform he seemed much diminished. There was a suggestion of emaciation in the tightly stretched skin, the sharpness of chin and nose, the prominence of his cheekbones.

Darrow's attitude toward the young officer for whom he had formed so strong an affection was almost paternal. Tommy was to be his witness for what he had called "the human element" in the case. He could have found no more dramatic a subject for psychological study—for public enlightenment, as well as for the law's condonation—of causes and motives.

"Do you remember going to a dance?"

Tommy's answer was fraught with unresolved terrors. "I can't forget it."

"That was in September of last year?"

"Yes."

"Where was the party?"

"At the Ala Wai Inn. That afternoon I asked Mrs. Massie if she'd like to go. She said she didn't care much about going, but that she would. We called up some friends to accompany us. After dinner she didn't feel like going, but I persuaded her to go."

Just as Kelley had feared he would, Darrow was going to take the witness all through the Ala Moana case, with all its causes and effects, its grievous impact on Tommy, its undeniable motivation for what followed. Kelley was at once on his feet to ask if counsel intended to go into the Ala Moana case.

Darrow, who had never actually admitted that this was to be a part of his strategy, replied blandly: "I do so intend."

Rejecting all subtlety, declining to be party to defense maneuvering for which he would be no match, Kelley demanded: "Then prosecution should therefore be allowed to know if an insanity plea is to be used."

Darrow answered with defensive vagueness. "We do expect to raise the question of the sanity of the moving one in the last part of this affair, the one who shot the pistol."

Kelley wanted no vagueness.

"We wish to know if the plea of insanity is to be offered in behalf of Lieutenant Massie."

"I don't see that is necessary," said Darrow.

Kelley thrust his full weight behind an angry objection. "I object to further examination of Lieutenant Massie on the Ala Moana case unless the defense intends to offer a plea of insanity for him."

"Inasmuch as the prosecution has linked all the defendants together as equally guilty," said Darrow coolly,

"I don't think it necessary at this time to point out any particular person."

Kelley protested vehemently, "The prosecution has the right to know the persons for whom the plea is to be made so that alienists for the prosecution may examine them."

Darrow's only concession to that protest was to invite the prosecution to have alienists in court to listen to the testimony and form their opinions on it. With this Kelley had to be satisfied according to a ruling by the Judge.

Prosecution alienists were brought into court. Alienists for the defense were already present. No one questioned the absurdity of psychiatry blowing hot or cold depending on whose side it was on.

Darrow resumed his examination of the witness. He was the venerable, kindly father-figure who saw Tommy, as he had seen so many before him, not as a defendant who must be punished for a crime in accordance with the law, but as a human being who may or may not have performed a certain act because of certain inducing causes. It was to these causes above all that he was dedicated. Sometimes he stood, sometimes he sat, ranging about the floor of the court—no different from the courts in which so many years of his life had been spent—to the atmosphere of which he had become as much inured as he was to his own living room. With all due respect to the bench, he knew that he was as much an officer of the court as the Judge. That his concept of justice or jurisprudence may have been different from that of the prosecution, could not change the fact that he was as much an officer of the court as was Kelley.

To Tommy, he now said: "You were proceeding to tell me about this dinner. There were other people at the dance?"

"Yes—a large crowd. Quite a few Navy people. We got there about nine-thirty."

Darrow brushed aside the thin lock of silvery hair which kept falling across the magnificent sweep of his brow.

"Was there any drinking there?"

"Yes—there was some. At eleven-thirty, Mrs. Rainier said it was time to go home. In the meantime, Lieutenant and Mrs. Rigby had invited us to drop in at their home. We couldn't find Mrs. Massie. We looked all over. I looked on the grounds and couldn't find her there. I thought she had gone home with Mrs. Rigby. We called several homes by phone, but couldn't locate her. We started out to the car, feeling sure she would be at Mrs. Rigby's."

This was a recital of the early events of that evening which Darrow was now hearing for perhaps the third or fourth time. He had also read it in the press on the mainland. He had read it in Admiral Stirling's report to the Secretary of the Navy. He now assumed from what Tommy had told from the witness stand that when Thalia could not be located, Tommy, as would any concerned husband, "started out to the car" at once. Certainly he did not feel it necessary to ask at what time Tommy had actually left the Inn. Nor did he feel it necessary to inquire any deeper into the reasons that Thalia had left the Inn. About the altercation in the private dining room, he apparently knew nothing. Nor did anyone feel that it was necessary to tell him.

He had taken the case, he had said, because the more he read about it, the stranger and more puzzling it became. It seemed now that it was no longer strange or puzzling. Certainly he did not act as though he were the victim of certain sins of omission.

"Was your wife especially fond of these parties?" he asked."

"No—I can't say that she was."

"Had she ever before left a party?"

"Yes—on several occasions when I was having a good time and didn't want to leave, she'd ask me to excuse her and go home."

Darrow was aware that many strange stories had circulated about the situation. They were often conflicting, and always sensational. Most of them, he felt sure, were highly improbable if not impossible. They had stemmed, it seemed to him, from the fact that Thalia had gone alone from the Ala Wai Inn. Apparently he saw nothing odd about that. As far as he knew, no one who was acquainted with Thalia had ever criticized her conduct, or had the slightest reason for suspicion of her behavior. He himself had none at all.

He asked Tommy, "What happened after you left the Inn?"

"Lieutenant Branson and I went to the Rigbys'—but no one was there. The maid said Mrs. Massie had not been there. I called my home and Mrs. Massie said: 'Something terrible has happened. Please come home!'

"When I got there she was crying, and collapsed in my arms. Blood was coming from her nose and mouth. Her lips were crushed and bruised, her eyes swollen. There was a large bruise on the right side of her face."

"Did she tell you what happened?"

"No. I thought a truck had run over her. I kept asking her and she said, 'It's too horrible.' She could only sob. I said 'Please tell me.' 'I can't. It's too terrible, too awful,' she said. She finally told me some men had dragged her into a car, beaten her, taken her to a place and—ravished her. I said, 'Oh my God, no!' "

How could anyone possibly doubt that this was what had happened—that this was what he had been told? His statement could not be doubted by Kelley; it could not be doubted by the jury. Seven months after the event it still had the power to thicken Tommy's voice with feeling, to dry his lips and cloud his eyes. Spellbound with horror, Mrs. Fortescue leaned forward to listen. It was as though she were hearing it for the first time. He was telling of her feelings as much as his own.

He went on: "I was stunned. She kept saying she wanted to die. I tried to comfort her and I couldn't. I called the police and told them to come at once. I got a towel and tried to get the blood away but she wouldn't let me. She just stayed in my arms and sobbed, completely broken. I asked her if she had taken precautions against conception and disease, and she said, 'Yes—everything I can.' The police came. Mrs. Massie said her jaw hurt frightfully and she couldn't talk. We wanted to go to the hospital, but the police stayed and questioned us. Finally another car came and she was taken to the hospital where they examined her. Then they took us to the police station. Lieutenant Branson was there and said he was being held as a suspect. I told the police to let him go, that he had been with me all evening."

(Lieutenant Branson was the officer who had been counted out by his fellow officers at the Ala Wai Inn that evening. Police had picked him up wandering drunkenly in Manoa Valley. He had apparently been on his way to the Massies from his own home.)

Darrow did not interrupt Tommy's account of that evening. Tommy continued: "Over and over she asked why the men hadn't killed her."

Next day, he said, a doctor told him that Thalia was in critical condition from mental and physical shock, possibly suffering from a broken jaw as well, and that she needed to be hospitalized.

The following day, while she was in the hospital, "the police brought in the four assailants."

Kelley broke his silence now by objecting to the use of the word "assailants." The word was changed to "persons."

"They [the police]," Tommy went on, "told Mrs. Massie not to show if she recognized them . . . She questioned them all but seemed to concentrate her questions on Kahahawai. After fifteen minutes, the detectives called me out and said, 'Go back and see what your wife says.' I leaned over the bed and she said, 'They are the ones.'

" 'Don't let there be any doubt of it,' I said. She said, 'Don't you know if there were any doubt I could never draw another easy breath?' "

Now, in the hushed and rigidly attentive courtroom, Tommy pictured the pain and terror of the days and nights which followed Thalia's return from the hospital.

"One night she rose up in bed and screamed, 'Don't let him get me.' I said, 'Nobody is here, darling, nobody but me.' 'Yes,' she cried, 'Kahahawai is here!'

"Friends advised me to go back to duty, to take my mind off it. I went back, but every time I was still, the whole thing came back to my mind and all I could see was that crushed face I had seen in September. I couldn't sleep. I used to get up and walk the floor, going over it again and again."

Moved though he was by the account, Darrow nonetheless remembered to ask: "Did you ever get it out of your mind?"

"Never! One night she called me and I heard footsteps under the window. There was no doubt about it. I ran out with a gun and circled the house, but couldn't see anyone.

"At the hospital, Dr. Porter [a naval surgeon] had said there were two things to expect—disease and conception."

"Might that pregnancy have been due to you?"

"No," said Tommy strongly, "it couldn't have been!"

Any questions as to why it couldn't have been were discreetly left unasked, and it was at this point that Tommy's first day on the witness stand ended. Mrs. Fortescue rushed up to him the moment court was adjourned. Arm-in-arm they left the courtroom. His testimony had touched all hearts, he had been magnificent, she seemed to be saying by her closeness. And it was true that his testimony had brought tears to the eyes of many of the Haole women who heard it.

Next day, Darrow was unable to appear in court. He was sick. A Navy doctor diagnosed his trouble as an intestinal upset. The jury was permitted to spend the day watching some tennis matches in the company of the court bailiff.

If Darrow's indisposition was an occupational hazard, it was also an opportunity for coming to a decision, for the next day when he appeared in court, fit and well, he began with a statement to the bench.

"Your Honor," he said, "there seems to be a little misunderstanding. The evidence shows that Lieutenant Massie, who is now on the stand, fired the fatal shot. We are willing to state, to avoid conflict in this court, that Lieutenant Massie held the gun when the fatal shot was fired."

This was an admission that he had hitherto been reluctant to make. It confirmed what Kelley already knew of Darrow's intention to plead insanity for Tommy. Yet he did not raise the issue until Darrow asked Tommy the result of the trial in the Ala Moana case, at which point he rose with a spirited objection.

"The only plea on which this testimony is admissible, is if it is to show the insanity of Massie or some other one of the defendants. We insist upon knowing this at this time."

The objection gave Darrow no choice but to show his hand, but in doing so he resorted to a tortuous tactic. He said: "Your Honor, I didn't say that Lieutenant

Massie killed the man, but that the gun was held in his hand when it was fired, whether or not he knew what he was doing."

This was splitting hairs with a vengeance. It was an answer which had provided the basis for many a courtroom joke on the guilt or innocence of a defendant. But Kelley was in no mood for jokes.

"Then we must ask," he rapped, "if the defendant is now sane."

It was the Judge who now came to Darrow's rescue by giving it as his opinion that he did not think it was necessary for the Court to rule on this.

Darrow seized on this ruling to ask the Court to presume that Lieutenant Massie was insane.

Now he could develop his premise that there is a degree of suffering which makes men mad enough to kill without knowing that they have killed!

TWENTY

The insidious spread of rumor, its pernicious effect, marked the beginning of Tommy's "insanity."

"The rumors were vile . . . rotten!"

These were value judgments which Kelley could easily have had stricken, but he chose to let them stand. The facts were still against the witness. Did all his suffering make him unaware of the difference between right and wrong? Kelley didn't think so.

Tommy had heard all the rumors. There was no way of not hearing them in a city as small as Honolulu, in a tight little community like Pearl Harbor.

"One was that I was getting a divorce. Another was that I went home the night of the dance and found my wife with Lieutenant Branson . . . and beat up my own wife. I also heard that I followed her in a car and beat her up, and that a crowd of naval officers had assaulted her. Another story was that my wife had never been assaulted at all . . .

"I got so I couldn't stand crowds, couldn't look people in the face. I felt miserable and couldn't sleep. I felt like I'd like to cut my brain out . . .

"Then I went to see a lawyer to ask how I could stop these terrible tales which were cracking my mind. He told me the best way was to get a confession signed by one of Mrs. Massie's assailants. He warned that force must not be used."

Now he told of how he and his mother-in-law had talked of ways to stop the rumors.

"I heard that Kahahawai was getting ready to crack. I told Major Ross about this, and I told him who I was. He said he would be glad to call Kahahawai in, and that he would talk to him as a former battalion commander [in Hawaii's National Guard, of which Kahahawai had been a member]. He said he would call me in a few days, but he did not. When I didn't hear from him, Mrs. Fortescue went down to learn what time the defendants came to the courthouse every day. We thought we might get one of them and bring him to the house and scare him into a confession."

"Did you have any intention to kill him?" asked Darrow.

Kelley objected to the question, but was overruled.

"No," said Tommy, "certainly not."

And now for the first time, since the prosecution had no firsthand knowledge of what had actually happened in the living room of Mrs. Fortescue's bungalow, the account of it was to come from the lips of one of the participants—to be believed or disbelieved by the millions who would hear it on their radios that same night—to be weighed and judged by the jury.

They were in the living room—the door closed and blocked by a chair—himself, Mrs. Fortescue, Lord and the seated Kahahawai. The gun was in Tommy's hand.

"Do you know who I am?" he had asked Kahahawai.

"I think so."

"I want the complete story of what happened. You did your lying in the courtroom, but you tell the truth now."

He had pulled back the slide of the .32 automatic and let it click back into place. The muzzle was aimed directly at the big Hawaiian's heart.

"I don't know nothing," Kahahawai said.

"You'd better tell the story. . . . When did you leave the dance and where did you pick up the woman?"

"We didn't have no woman."

"You had better tell the truth. Who kicked the woman?"

"Nobody kicked her."

"Now I know you are lying."

"I don't know nothing," Kahahawai still insisted.

To frighten him (apparently the gun was not menace enough, since he had said he had no intention to kill him), Tommy told Lord to go out and get the boys.

To Kahahawai he said: "Ida talked and he told plenty

on you. Those men will beat you to ribbons. You know your gang was there."

It was at this point, according to Tommy, that Kahahawai, apparently more afraid of a beating than of the gun, broke down and admitted: "Yeah—we done it!"

All that Tommy could remember after that was the picture in his mind of Thalia being assaulted and begging for mercy, and Kahahawai striking her in the face.

"Then what did you do?" Darrow asked him.

But his mind was a blank. "I don't remember."

"What became of the gun?"

He did not know.

"Where was Lord?"

"He had gone outside and slammed the door to carry out our bluff."

"Do you remember the flight to the mountains?"

"No."

"What's the first thing you recall?"

"I remember being in a car on a country road."

"Who was driving?"

"I don't remember."

"Do you remember who was with you?"

"No. I think I remember a bunch of people coming up to us. Some were in uniform and they were talking about a body."

"Do you remember any of these people?"

"I think I do."

"Do you remember being taken to the police station?"

"I think I do."

Darrow ended the examination abruptly at that moment. It may have occurred to him that Tommy's inability to remember (the same sort of inability which had affected Thalia when she was on the witness stand in the earlier trial, and his mother-in-law when she made a statement to the public prosecutor) did not apply to the moment when he had shaken hands with himself in front of the radio patrol officer on the Koko Head Road. Naturally he would have preferred that entire incident to be forgotten.

Kelley's cross-examination of Tommy began with an attempt to gain an admission from him that he was proud of being a Southerner. It was not a particularly tactful gambit, and it was quickly objected to by Darrow, and just as quickly stricken.

Kelley was no father-figure to whom Tommy could unburden himself of his torment, to whom he could admit holding the gun, menacing Kahahawai with it, threatening him with savagery if he would not talk. Kelley was no man of pity and mercy who would understand and forgive. He would forgive nothing, would understand only what it served his purpose to understand.

All his questions were aimed toward the fulfillment of that purpose. Tommy's answers were abrupt, embittered, defensive.

Did he remember Mrs. Fortescue telling a reporter that they had bungled the job?

No!

Had he ever had spells before?

He had fainted once after bleeding internally following an operation.

"Did Kahahawai seem frightened?"

"Yes."

"Did he plead for mercy?"

"No."

"Did he put up any fight?"

"No."

Like a pool player pocketing one ball after another, Kelley was pocketing answers and setting up the remaining questions in positions which would enable him to pocket the big answer to the vital question of just when did Tommy's mind snap.

He was in no hurry. He would come back to it presently.

At a tangent he asked: "You stated here that your wife had walked out on other parties?"

Tommy resented the implication. "I said she had excused herself—not walked out!"

"Did she ever leave a party at Diamond Head and go home alone?"

"Not that I remember."

"She did not leave this party [at the Ala Wai Inn] because of your condition?"

"I hope not."

Although Tommy had admitted earlier that he had

brought a pint bottle of liquor to the Inn, he had denied that he was drunk. But his answer, despite his arch denial that Thalia would leave a party because of his condition, was not as positive as it could have been. It seemed to be a little evasive.

Unexpectedly, Kelley asked: "Since you came to Honolulu have you engaged in amateur plays?"

If the question was designed to elicit the information that Tommy was a pretty good actor, both on the stage and on the witness stand, it failed.

As rueful as he was ingenuous, Tommy said: "Yes—unfortunately. I was in 'Meet the Wife' once, in which I forgot my lines at an important place. That was a year ago."

"Was that a naval play?"

"Naval personnel, yes."

Kelley quickly dropped the curtain on this speculative venture into the performing arts.

He came back to Kahahawai. Tommy, in his examination by Darrow, had told of hearing that the Hawaiian was about to crack. Had he not also heard, Kelley asked him, that Kahahawai had consistently refused to confess?

Tommy hadn't heard. In fact: "I was usually the last one to get things . . . as the husband always is."

This could have been locker room humor. It could also have been a disenchanted facet of a kind of Hemingway syndrome, the sort of thing that a peacetime naval officer like Tommy might have envied. Perhaps he longed for the enduring simplicities. Like Hemingway's heroes he wanted love, affection, loyalty, mirth—to quote an observer of that time. The complex feelings roused by betrayal, by sudden death, could not be dealt with except by the gallant laughter of Hemingway's lost generation.

Kelley was now back at the pool table. He wanted to know whether Tommy knew who had stripped Kahahawai's body.

He knew only because he was told, Tommy said.

"Who told you?"

"Jones."

"What did he tell you?"

"That the stains wouldn't come out, so they took his clothes off. I think that's what he told me."

Now Kelley's questioning became an attempt to discover what he was told and what he knew for himself.

"Did anyone tell you about washing the clothes in the bathtub?"

"No—I don't think so."

"Did anyone tell you where he died?"

"Yes—Mrs. Fortescue. It was on the chaise lounge."

"Did anyone tell you how long it took him to die?"

"No."

"Did they tell you about taking him to the bathroom?"

"Yes—I think so."

"Were you told how the body was taken to the sedan?"

"Yes."

"And what their purpose was?"

"They said they were all so excited they were running around in circles. I presume Jones and Lord carried the body out."

The jury was left to visualize the frenzied, nightmare scene, the "running around in circles." Did they wonder whether the seamen and Mrs. Fortescue were giving Tommy blow-by-blow reports on their hectic activities? Would he have understood in his amnesiac condition? Were they aware of that condition?

"Kahahawai was a heavy man, wasn't he?"

"Jones and Lord are strong men," said Tommy, implying of course that his own help wasn't needed.

"Do you remember getting into the sedan?"

"No—for all I know I might have gone to China. Mrs. Fortescue said Jones pushed me into it."

"Did Jones ever say why he didn't go along?"

"Yes. Mrs. Fortescue had told him to straighten up the house."

Kelley did not have the vital answer, in so many words, as to just when Tommy's mind went blank. But he seemed fairly well satisfied with what he had accomplished so far.

There was still a little more, however.

"Lieutenant Massie, were you ever told by any of the defendants what happened to the gun you had in your hand?"

"Yes. Jones said he left it at my house."

"Did anyone ever tell you who took it away from your house?"

"No. They wouldn't tell me."

"Did anyone tell you what you did after the shot was fired?"

"Mrs. Fortescue said I just stood there and wouldn't talk. She took me into the kitchen and tried to get me to drink some oke, but I wouldn't take it."

"What did Jones say?"

"Jones wasn't very complimentary."

In a rare burst of sarcasm, Kelley snorted, asking, "Why? Because you only shot him once?"

Tommy's sense of humor must have deserted him, for he answered: "No—he said I acted like a damn fool."

Still sarcastic, Kelley pretended surprise: "Yet he's an enlisted man!"

"Yes—and I resented it," said Tommy. Then, with almost puerile righteousness he added: "Lord never said anything to me about my actions."

Kelley stared at him, not knowing what to make of a man whose brilliantly calculated sophistry had been reduced to absurdity by waspish indignation, querulous hurt because an enlisted man had called him a damn fool. Even the fact that he was a fellow conspirator, a codefendant, didn't give him the right to say that to a superior officer!

There was no wit in Kelley to match this pitiful irrelevance.

He asked: "Did Mrs. Fortescue tell you about the trip to Koko Head?"

"Yes," said Tommy. "She said they wanted to go to the sea to dispose of the body."

When or where she had told him of that desperate and ill-fated expedition remained a mystery.

There was a moment now when Kelley, tiring perhaps of this battle for Tommy's mind, as it were, turned to an incident in the past.

He wanted to know whether Tommy had once before been implicated in a kidnapping. A kidnapping? Tommy was bewildered. Where? When?

Kelley reminded him, asking him whether he had ever

assisted in kidnapping a baby at Patchogue, Long Island, while visiting the then Miss Fortescue.

Angered, Tommy retorted: "I was not implicated in any kidnapping of a baby, never have and never will be!"

"Were you arrested?"

Before Tommy could answer, Darrow rose to object, although it was obvious that until this moment he had known nothing of the incident. The judge overruled the objection . . . and Tommy went on to explain:

"Miss Fortescue, now Mrs. Massie, and I went to a movie at Patchogue, and when we came out there was a little baby sitting by the ticket box in a carriage, crying.

"Mrs. Massie said something about 'Oh, poor little thing; I will roll it down a block and maybe it will hush crying.'

"When we got halfway down the block, a woman came screaming and shouting and said, 'You are kidnapping my baby!' I think she was an Italian woman and she came up to Mrs. Massie and said, 'Well, you give me five dollars and I won't say anything about this.' Mrs. Massie laughed at her.

"Next morning police held an investigation and dismissed the charge you call kidnapping."

Well, that was Tommy's scornful version of the affair. Kelley had no witnesses with whom to discredit it. He let it pass.

What he had, perhaps, was a newspaper account of the incident. The headline ran:

A FOOLISH PRANK! THALIA FORTESCUE WALKED OFF WITH BABY LEFT IN THEATRE LOBBY!

It then reported the incident in the characteristic style of a small town editorial. The story was date-lined August 26, 1927:

While a sense of humor is often a saving grace and helps to brighten the dull path of life in a busy, humdrum existence, still the question of just what is a good joke depends more or less on one's point of view.

When Miss Thalia Fortescue, the sixteen-year-old daughter

of Mr. and Mrs. Granville Fortescue of Bayport, spied a baby asleep in a carriage in the lobby of the Patchogue Theatre on Wednesday evening, she suggested to Thomas F. Massie, age 22, an ensign on the U.S.S. Lexington, by whom she was accompanied, that it would be lots of fun to take the baby out of his carriage and take him for a walk about the streets of Patchogue.

It did not seem so funny however when pursued by the baby's frantic mother and irate father, to whom the disappearance of the baby had been reported by the manager of the theatre. . . . Miss Fortescue and Massie were arrested. . . . . Later in the evening however, when the case was heard before Police Justice August D. Schoenfeld Jr., the young couple convinced the baby's father that they were merely indulging in a youthful prank and the charge was . . . dismissed . . .

This was not how Tommy had remembered it. But in recalling his version, had he perhaps remembered more? Had he remembered that he was unmarried then? That his career as a Navy officer had hardly begun? Was there a fleeting moment of regret for what might have been had he never met Thalia? By what strange passivity did a man yield to a sixteen-year-old's whim, to her mother's intrigue?

Nothing in his manner indicated that these questions had occurred to him. There was a more immediate peril to preoccupy his mind, the mind over which a merciful darkness had apparently descended at the moment the fatal shot was fired.

There were experts in court who would now give their opinions on the authenticity of that darkness.

TWENTY-ONE

Not yet had it been written that "the mind is a something with such manifold variety, such fleeting changes, such countless nuances, such wealth of combinations, such heights and depths of mood, such sweeps of passion . . ."

This was to come eight years later from the pen of a great biologist.

Now it was for the alienists to say what was in the mind of Lieutenant Massie before and after the alleged inciting admission, "Yeah—we done it!"

Their profession was still largely in its infancy. The great sweep of psychiatry into the everyday language of America was a decade and more away. It would depend on the jury's comprehension whether or not the opinions of the alienists would have any bearing on the outcome of the trial. And it very soon became apparent that diagnostic evaluations varied with the diagnostician, not with the ailment.

Tommy had indeed suffered from insanity at the time the bullet was fired in the opinion of Dr. Thomas J. Orbison of Los Angeles.

The doctor, a ruddy, bespectacled, well-fed man, who wore a hearing-aid, now elaborated on this opinion. He described Tommy's kind of insanity as "delirium with ambulatory automatism."

There was room for much semantic confusion in a phrase of this kind, but Darrow, whose witness the doctor was, seemed to know exactly what he meant. He asked the doctor to tell the court what the first inducing cause of this illness might be.

"The ravishing of his wife would be the first," said the doctor.

"What else?"

"Well—he said he carried around this terrible idea for months. His attitude toward rumors, the things he heard on the street. He told me, for instance, that the story was around that his wife had not been assaulted at all. Tears came to his eyes when he said it was rumored that he himself had struck her in the jaw. Things of that character he was hearing all the time."

The doctor now explained that "a protracted worry might bring out an actively irritated condition, resulting in pouring a secretion into the blood which would cause a nervous condition. Strong emotion would have an important effect on the supra-renal glands."

To avoid any suggestion to the jury that Tommy's trouble might be nothing more than a kidney complaint, Darrow quickly led the doctor back to the real issue.

"You have said by your examination that the defendant was insane prior to and after the shooting."

"He became insane at the moment he heard the last words of Kahahawai," said Dr. Orbison confidently. "He was under a strain he had never been subjected to before and had been thwarted in his attempts to clear his wife's character. He was agitated daily for months, and at times he could scarcely bear it. People had asked him why he didn't kill the assailants. He said 'If I told you why I didn't plan anything of the kind, you wouldn't understand.' I said, 'I am older than you and I think I can understand.'

"There were three things that kept him back, he told me. 'It had been grounded into my soul to observe law ever since I had been in the Navy,' he said. Another thing was that Admiral Stirling had told him to do nothing that might spoil the situation. But his strongest motive was, he said, to get some kind of confession that could be used to clear the whole question."

Kelley, although he had listened carefully, preferred to leave the cross-examination of the experts to Barry Ulrich.

"Is it not true," Ulrich asked the doctor, "that you've expressed the opinion that Lieutenant Massie did not know what he was doing because he told you he did not know?"

"No."

"Is it true that your opinion is based on an assumption that what he told you was true?"

"No."

"Is it possible that a man might go through this stress and in a fit of anger might kill a man and know it?"

The doctor, well aware of all the booby-trapped entanglements of forensic medicine—of the McNaghten Rule whereby guilt or innocence was determined on the basis of the defendant's knowledge of the difference between right and wrong—promptly explained: "That condition you call anger would be anger with a delirium that is defined as insanity."

"You think it improbable that he killed him in a fit of anger?"

"Yes—because all his plans under this stress led up to getting a confession . . . and he killed the very person necessary to this purpose."

This, in the doctor's opinion, was insanity. It could also, provided Kahahawai had actually confessed, have been the action of a man who in a moment of triumph flees into failure because that is the deeper root of his nature.

A second expert was called by the defense—Dr. Edward H. Williams—stolid, professionally serious. He wore a Van Dyke beard, sported a polka-dotted bow tie.

"Lieutenant Massie," he announced unequivocally, "was legally and actually insane," when the shot was fired.

His insanity, Dr. Williams went on to say, was not emotional, but chemical, arising from a chemical shock producing amnesia.

Unimpressed, the prosecution wanted to know the duration of this chemically induced amnesia. The police had testified that when Tommy was asked to make a statement soon after his capture, he declined. Was he still in a state of amnesia at that point?

"He might have been coming out of it," said the doctor without a moment's hesitation. "The statement is perfectly normal."

"Then he was normal?"

"No," said the doctor promptly. "The statement was."

This glib separation of the man from his words could hardly have been convincing to the jury. One even doubts whether it was convincing to Darrow.

A Dr. Paul Bowers, called by the prosecution, took a

dim view of Tommy's insanity. The killing of Kahahawai, he said was "a logical sequence of the plan."

He outlined the sequence, but not before first complaining that the defense had not allowed him to interview Tommy.

"The individuals," he said, "knowing the consequences, took deliberate steps toward self-protection. There may have been a spirit of vengeance such as exists in certain persons feeling that they have not obtained justice by legal means. The individual measured ways and considered the nature and consequences of his act. The steps of the plan were securing the automobile, wearing gloves and goggles, being prepared with guns, and taking steps for disposing of the body.

"At no time in reading the records of this case did I find any evidence or any symptoms of insanity, and I conclude that that individual was in a normal state of consciousness at the time of the crime."

It was during the testimony of the second expert for the prosecution that Darrow, in cross-examining him, a Dr. Joseph Catton, Associate Professor of Medicine at Stanford University, revealed that he was not altogether happy with the way the expert testimony was going.

All at once, he attacked the doctor's deportment.

"I object to the witness's manner," he grumbled irritably. "Why doesn't he sit in the chair like any other witness instead of addressing the jury? If he is going to do that he might as well get up and make a speech to them. That is not the attitude of an impartial—"

The witness, crimsoning with anger, exploded: "Do you mean to insinuate that I am not honest? I resent it!"

Indifferently, Darrow growled: "Well, resent it, then!"

The experts had demonstrated, it seemed, that integrity aside, it was he who paid their fees who called the psychiatric tune.

Tommy's insanity was still open to question. Darrow knew now that it would take much more compelling testimony than that of the experts to win his case.

TWENTY-TWO

Darrow had perhaps hoped that it would not be necessary—
that there would come a point in the trial when he would
know, experienced advocate that he was, that the portents
were favorable. But now that he had been "watching and
catching all that goes on in a trial" he knew that he could
no longer delay calling a witness whom he would have
preferred not to call. He called Thalia.

The trial had taken on some of the atmosphere of a
social event. Like the Roman aristocracy who came to
watch the gladiators, Honolulu's *kamaaina* elite came to
this tropical arena to watch their brave gladiator destroy
the prosecution to the glory of white supremacy.

A flip, but lackluster gossip column in a Haole daily
simpered delightedly over their presence:

Mrs. Jean Beck, alert as a bird in the rear row of spectators.

In the nine to ten o'clock session, strains of music floated
through the windows from the direction of the palace square.

Among the "regulars" were Mrs. George P. Cooke, Mrs.
Rudolph Bukely, Mrs. Harry Kluegel, Mrs. Walter Wall, Miss
Alice Wall, Mrs. Harry Bent, Mrs. Walter Dillingham.

When Clarence Darrow rises to speak in court, his left hand
slips into his coat pocket while his right knuckles touch the
table, or he toys with his glasses.

The columnist undoubtedly saw omens of victory in
Darrow's mannerisms. He had become the darling of the
Haoles.

Thalia's arrival at the Judiciary Building in the Navy car which brought Tommy and Mrs. Fortescue to Court each day was greeted with breathless excitement and admiration by the Haoles. Crowds surrounded the car. Flash bulbs popped. The path to the courtroom was lined with fans, for to them she was the star of the show.

Unlike Tommy, she had put on some weight in the months of seclusion. Her round face was heavier. Instead of the youthful impermanence there was a kind of soft maturity. There was a suggestion of melancholy in the remoteness of her gaze, as though disenchantment had taken a firm hold.

Not as a plaintiff now, but as a witness called in defense of a husband charged with second-degree murder, she was to repeat the story she had told in the Ala Moana case—not to accuse, but to condone.

The same ironic turn of events which had compelled Admiral Stirling to defend rather than attack, which had transformed the drive of the entire white community from a passion for punishment into a passion for acquittal, had now entangled Thalia.

Darrow was aware of the dangers he faced in calling her. She had told the story so often. It was possible that by its very repetition a great deal of its emotional horror would be lost, that she would be so detached from it as to sound unconvincing to the jury.

She had been seated next Tommy, holding hands with him, when her name was called. Now she walked to the stand, a young, rather expressionless woman wearing a black crepe dress with a loose, green and white-dotted coatee, still prey to the awkward slouch of her shoulders. A scar was noticeable on her jaw. She sat and faced the man who would have to demand expression of feeling from one who was perhaps no longer capable of it.

Darrow opened with the slow, settling foreplay of identification, soothing her with the innocent formalities of name and age and address.

Then: "Do you remember the night at the Inn?"

There were a number of ways in which to interpret the blink of her eyes before she answered "Yes"—as fear, as uncertainty, as an ineffectual response to the emotion that was expected of her.

Now, in substance if not in words, she repeated the story of her departure from the Inn. She had left at 11:35, because she was not enjoying the party; planned to walk to the corner and back.

No sooner had Darrow asked her where she was when "something unusual happened," than Kelley was on his feet with a violent objection.

"The only pertinent question is about what she told her husband! We are not trying the Ala Moana case!"

There was something like a hiss from the Haole claque in the courtroom as Darrow was forced to yield to the objection.

"When did you next see Tom?"

"Later on that night."

"What happened then?"

Suddenly she was in tears. Darrow was surprised. He had hardly expected tears so soon, if at all. He could regret that it was necessary to shed them, but he was relieved that they had come. After all, the suffering of this young wife was a clear vindication of his belief that this whole trial was a question of "causes and motives."

Surely what had happened to her that night would be more than enough to "cause and motivate" an insane rage in a husband!

Tears did not impair her recall of what she had told Tommy that night.

"I told Tommy that they had raped me and that Kahahawai had broken my jaw. He hit me as hard as he could. He would not let me pray. I said 'You will knock my teeth out!' Kahahawai said: 'What do I care? Shut up!' "

The others stood around and laughed. One held her arm. Then another one assaulted her.

Her beads had been found near the old quarantine station. Police had found some of her beads in the Ida car.

While this was something that she may have been told and which she, in turn, told Tommy, the truth was that in attempting to secure a confession from Ida, a police officer had told him of finding some of the beads in his car. Ida's reply to that had been to say that "If you found beads in my car, then it's a frameup!"

Nonetheless, Thalia was giving the jury everything that Darrow expected of her, not only in the description of her own ordeal, but of the shattering effect it had on Tommy.

Yet he was noble, withal.

"Tommy never complained about the many times I would wake him at night. He was wonderful. He was so fine . . . He never wanted to go out. He did not sleep, had rings around his eyes, and would get up at night and walk up and down the living room smoking cigarettes."

It was all Tommy's anguish now, as Darrow led her carefully through her account of it.

"When I got so I could cook, I would prepare tempting dishes for him, but he would not eat; he would get up and smoke a cigarette."

Was it enough—this moving description of a man's agony by a loyal and loving wife, who put her husband's ordeal above her own? Darrow believed that it was.

The seaman Jones had been arrested at her home on the morning of the murder. Darrow, too eager perhaps to scotch any suspicion that Thalia may have been implicated in the murder, asked her when he had come.

"He came around ten o'clock."

"Was it before the killing?"

"No, after."

"What was his condition?"

"He came in and called excitedly. He handed me a gun and said, 'Here, take this. Kahahawai has been killed.' I said, 'Where is Tommy?' He said he had sent Tommy off with Mother. He asked for a drink and I fixed him a highball."

Had he indeed exonerated her? She had performed nobly for him. There was nothing more she could tell the jury. He could now allow Kelley to cross-examine.

Kelley charged directly into the opening which Darrow had left him, ignoring tears and emotional exhaustion, indifferent to the muttering of the Haole claque about which the Judge had already had occasion to warn them.

"Do you remember Captain McIntosh and the police coming to your house?"

"Yes."

"Did a telephone call come that was answered by Jones?"

She sat stiff, resentful, answering stonily.

"No."

"You're quite sure?"

"Yes."

"Was Jones sober when he arrived?"

"Yes."

"When you came out of the bedroom, he had already helped himself to a drink?"

"No. I came out as soon as he called me."

"Was he nervous?"

"He was excited."

"How many drinks did he take? Three or four?"

She flung back: "No—five or six! I made one and he said it wasn't strong enough and poured more in. Then he poured several more himself."

Jones, listening to this exchange, lowered his head modestly. He seemed to be secretly enjoying this description of his drinking capacity.

"After McIntosh came did you talk to your maid?"

"No."

"After they left?"

"Yes."

Her answer had come reluctantly.

And now he made the blunt accusation: "You told her to say Jones came about eight-thirty."

"No. I told her to say she was there when he came. She gets there at eight or eight-thirty."

She had told Darrow that Jones had come around ten o'clock. This was true. Now, in wrenching the admission from her that she had attempted to conspire with the maid to change the time of his arrival, she was disclosing the same ability to change facts to suit her own needs that she had shown in the Ala Moana trial.

The disclosures of this duality mounted.

"Do you remember Jones going to the telephone after you had answered it and asking, 'Who is calling?'"

"No!"

"Do you remember that Jones went to the telephone and said, 'Leo—cover him up!'?"

She did not remember that either.

Had she herself used those words, he asked.

Of course she hadn't. Had she used any? The answer was literally dragged from her.

"I just told Lieutenant [Leo] Pace, to stall them off

until I could find Tommy. I didn't know just what it was all about at the time."

The last sentence was almost too defensive. She was not a defendant.

Pitilessly, Kelley demanded: "Did you hear him [Jones] speak to Lieutenant Pace and say, 'Leo, cover him up?' "

She skirted the issue superciliously, "No—he would not address an officer by his first name"—an irrelevance almost as preposterous as her husband's, save that it indirectly answered the question.

Her whole manner had changed in the course of the cross-examination. Her answers had become petulant, biting. It could have taken very little more for her to have slapped Kelley as she had once slapped the officer who called her a louse.

Kelley had returned to his table to pick up a document which he studied for a moment before returning to the battle with his hostile witness. As far as he was concerned the battle was over. All that was necessary was to administer the coup de grâce.

Darrow did not know what was in the document. Its introduction was to take Thalia completely by surprise.

Quite irrelevantly, it seemed, he was asking blandly, "Did you ever have a psychopathic examination at the University of Hawaii?"

So unexpected was it that she answered almost without thinking, "I did."

Now he handed her the document: "Is this your handwriting?"

She stared at it, confused, angry, afraid.

She snapped: "This is a confidential matter! How did you get it?"

"I'm not answering questions," Kelley said.

There was a creaking of discomfort in the public section of the courtroom—someone coughed—then silence. They waited for her to answer the question. A psychopathic examination? Why? What did it mean? Both Tommy and Thalia's mother seemed as puzzled as the rest.

She held it in her hands. How ridiculous to call it a psychopathic examination! It wasn't that at all. She wasn't mentally ill. But Kelley—with his snide insinuations—had made it seem that she was. It was really nothing but a personality quiz. Women's magazines carried them all the time. Your score would tell you how well you knew yourself.

But it was a private matter, confidential. He would not even tell her how he got hold of it.

Suddenly she burst out: "This is a matter between a patient and a doctor. You have no right to bring it into open court. I refuse to answer."

Before Kelley could remind her that it was hardly a matter between patient and doctor, she tore the document apart, then in a kind of methodical fury, ripped it to shreds.

Kelley stood transfixed. Into the stunned silence broke the applause of the Haole claque. Darrow, who had never expected to meet such a document in court, could only bow his head. Tommy joined in the applause, perhaps because it was something the women were doing, and in his gallantry he could only follow suit.

The Judge demanded order. The applause died down. Kelley stared at the scattered fragments of the document. Then, drawing all the melodramatic nourishment he could from the incident, he nodded his head slowly as he looked at Thalia, savoring a moment of quiet triumph, and murmured: "Thank you, Mrs. Massie. You have revealed yourself in your true colors."

Darrow rose like an avenging angel to cry: "Strike that from the record!"

It was stricken. Kelley was rebuked by the Judge. No sooner had he announced that he had no further questions, than Tommy hurried to the witness stand. Thalia was sobbing now:

"What right had he to say that I don't love you? Everybody knows I love you!"

Unwittingly she had revealed the disturbing content of the document. Tommy kissed her. It seemed to be a kiss of understanding for the young girl who sought, but had still failed, to find an identity of her own.

Mrs. Fortescue dabbed at her eyes, momentarily isolated from their intimacy.

TWENTY-THREE

The temper of the trial was all in his favor now, Darrow believed. The document should never have been introduced by the prosecution. How could there be anything but overwhelming admiration for Thalia's courage in tearing it to pieces?

It did not seem to occur to those who had praised the act that it would have been more courageous to admit that it was hers, let Kelley read what it contained, then tell the Court that despite what she may have written, she still loved Tommy.

But that would have required the kind of courage that could withstand not only the avid curiosity of those who heard her, but also the emotional punishment of her own guilty feelings. It was all too much for her youth.

Darrow might wonder whether Thalia had later told Tommy what was in the document, but he would not wonder whether they had quarrelled about it. As far as he knew they had never quarrelled. Even if they had, he would have understood it as a forgivable aspect of human imperfection.

The only important thing now was their testimony, Thalia's and Tommy's.

To Darrow, as he now reviewed the transcript of all the testimony and prepared to deliver his closing argument, the case had resolved itself into a question of what a husband and mother were justified in doing. It was a contest over the question of "whether it was a duty to obey the

149

dead letter of the law, or the living emotions upon which
all life rests."

He preferred to minimize the fact that he had hoped
to base his defense on a plea of insanity.

The "trial-sitters" had begun to form a line in front of
the Judiciary Building at four in the morning on the day
Darrow was to address the jury. From darkness on, during
the previous night, they had camped on the Palace grounds,
a few hoping to get in themselves, but most expecting to
sell their places in line for prices which had now risen to
a $25 minimum.

Of that momentous session in court, from which he
would have allowed nothing short of a national emergency
to keep him away, Admiral Stirling said that Darrow's
figure, his coat hanging loosely about his bony frame,
breathed kindliness and sympathy to all. "The courtroom
seemed pervaded with his gentle, old voice. Its soothing
effect upon the courtroom was miraculous to see. Slowly
his voice was stamping out all bitterness."

This was hardly the Darrow of an earlier day, the man
whose voice and opinions electrified and disturbed, who
shattered the idols of conformity with a blast of fury at
the law's inhumanity.

Had he now reached a stage in his career when it was
more comfortable to tranquilize rather than agitate?

At about nine-thirty that morning of April 27, 1932—
more than three weeks after the trial had begun—he began
to address the jury.

"Gentlemen, we are getting close to the end of this
case. It has been a long, serious, tedious trial, and you of
the jury probably have had the worst of it."

His voice was sad rather than gentle at the outset.
He moved about before the jury, hands in pockets or an
arm raised to stress a point, his deep-set eyes, still clear
and piercing, fixing one, then another, trying to reach
behind the mass of testimony to the core of their understanding.

"This case illustrates the working of human destiny more
than any other case I have handled. It illustrates the effect
of sorrow and mishap on human minds and lives, and shows

us how weak and powerless human beings are in the hands of relentless powers."

The jury listened to the "soothing," philosophical and profoundly human substance of his words. He was playing, as he himself would be the first to admit, on the emotions of his listeners. This he had always done, for it was his belief that men acted through emotions anyway. It was one of the secrets of his power to sway juries that he told them frankly, "I am not bound to believe them right in order to take their case, and you are not bound to believe them right in order to find them not guilty."

Right or wrong was not the fulcrum by which to determine guilt or innocence, in his philosophy. The issue was justice, real justice, the principal components of which were mercy, charity and understanding.

"Is there a more terrible story anywhere in literature?" he asked, once he had described the events of that September night, when in a few steps the lives of Tommy and Thalia Massie had gone from safety to destruction.

"The police were called to pick up the trail. No one raised even a doubt about this story, except the originators of a few vile slanders which were carried from tongue to tongue. Has anybody placed their finger upon a single fact to contradict the saddest tale that was ever brought to a husband . . . ?

"There have been people who spread around in this community stories I don't believe true. They concocted these terrible stories, and what effect did they have on Massie? May I ask . . ."—his gaze roamed the panel, resting on white and dark-skinned juror alike—"what effect they would have on you, and how you would have stood them?

"Our insane institutions are filled with men and women who had less cause for insanity than he had. Everyone knows it. The mind isn't too easy to understand at the best. But what happens to the human mind? It does one thing with one person and another thing with another. You know what it did to Massie's. Do you think he is responsible, or has been, from that terrible night?"

Although it had not been established that any evidence of disease or pregnancy was found in Thalia, Darrow portrayed in all its horror, the effect of either on a man like Tommy.

"Here is a man—his wife . . . she is bearing inside of her the germs of—who? Does anybody know? Not he . . . but some one of the ruffians who assaulted her and left a wreck of her. The doctor was not only a physician, but a friend. He asked no questions. He didn't even read the statutes. He wasn't afraid the district attorney would indict him for abortion. You know what a friend would do, what an intelligent physician would do. So he took away what was there. He did it out of kindness and consideration . . ."

He was baffled, Darrow told the jury. He could not understand why the jury disagreed in the Ala Moana case. He could not see why they had done so when the evidence was so strong, the facts so incontrovertible. He could not understand why months went by and the case was still not retried, he said. Then, apparently out of the clear air, he said, and with nothing on which to rest, strange, slanderous stories were spread over these islands about Lieutenant Massie and his ravished wife.

From under the perplexed set of crumpled eyebrows, his eyes, laced about in a network of wrinkles, hung on the non-Haole members of the jury: Chinese, part-Hawaiian, Portuguese. Had the disagreement of the Ala Moana jury baffled them too? Did they feel as he did? Was he reaching them?

He had looked so often at the faces of jurors on the mainland, caught their response to his oratory. It had refreshed and enlivened him. Yet here in half the members of the panel, there was only inscrutability. Possibly they did not appreciate the mores of the white world, the abiding oneness of husband and wife.

Would they understand a mother's oneness with her child? Surely that was universal.

He glanced over at Mrs. Fortescue. With a tiny, appealing movement of her head she communicated, tell them, make them understand!

"Here is a mother," he said. "What about her? They wired to her and she came. Poems and rhymes have been written about mothers. I don't want to bring forth further eulogies which are more or less worthwhile, but I want to call your attention to something more primitive than that. Nature. It is the case of what nature has done. I don't care whether it is human mother, a mother of beasts or birds of the air, they are all alike."

This was the cry of Charmian London. Now it was Darrow's. Hers had been a cry of outrage. His was a cry for understanding.

"To them there is one all-important thing, and that is a child that they carried in their womb. Without that feeling, which is so strong in all life, there would be no life preserved upon this earth. She acted as every mother acts. She felt as your mothers have felt, because the family is the preservation of life . . . I don't care if a mother is seventy-five and her daughter fifty, it is still mother and child . . .

"If this husband and this mother and these faithful boys go to the penitentiary, it won't be the first time that a penitentiary has been sanctified by its inmates."

The faces of the non-Haole jurors remained as inscrutable as ever. If there was response behind these masks, he could not detect it.

For some reason, he turned suddenly on Kelley.

"My amiable friend, the prosecutor—I almost said persecutor—" A relenting but still grim smile modified his bitterness. He added: "You're an Irishman; you can't be much in favor of persecution."

But his scorn was just as biting.

"Five years ago, before Massie and his wife were married, they went to a picture show and saw a baby in a carriage with flies bothering it. They trundled it a few blocks and were accused of kidnapping!" He threw up his hands. "They can't turn around without trouble! The only safe place for Massie was in a submarine. But the next day the case was dismissed."

He ripped into Kelley, the "persecutor."

"My God—what are you thinking of?" He spun back to the jury. "Yet that prank is paraded in this court because it might possibly turn the balance and put Massie and Mrs. Fortescue in prison!" Now he turned back to Kelley and with all his majestic and withering wrath cried: "There are some things even prosecutors shouldn't do, and that was one of them!"

Ten years earlier, Edgar Lee Masters, a former law partner

of Darrow's, who had given up law for literature, had
written a poetic fragment about him:

> This is a man with an old face, always old.
> There was pathos, in his face, and in his eyes,
> And early weariness; and sometimes tears in his eyes,
> Which he let slip unconsciously on his cheek,
> Or brushed away with an unconcerned hand.
> There were tears for human suffering, or for a glance
> Into the vast futility of life,
> Which he had seen from the first, being old
> When he was born.

Indeed the face was old, and the early weariness had
finally come to its natural time. But there was no glancing
into the vast futility of life as he fought for the defendants.
He gave their lives purpose.

"Gentlemen, you are asked to send these people to the
penitentiary. Do you suppose that if you had been caught
in the hands of Fate, would you have done differently? No,
we are not made that way. Life doesn't come that way.

"It comes from a devotion of mothers, of husbands,
loves of men and women, that's where life comes from.
Without this love, this devotion, the world will be desolate and cold and will take its lonely course around the
sun alone!

"Without a human heartbeat, there will be nothing
except thin air. Every instinct that moves human beings,
every feeling that is with you or any of your kin, every
feeling that moves in the mother of the animal is with us
in this case. You can't fight against it. If you do you are
fighting against nature and life . . .

"All right gentlemen, you have the power, but let me
say to you—that if on top of all else that has been heaped
upon the devoted heads of this family, if they should be
sent to prison, it would place a blot upon the fair name
of these Islands that all the Pacific seas would never wash
away!"

The blot was an understatement. Although he may not
have intended it that way, he was reminding the jury of
white repercussions should the defendants be sent to prison.
Kelley was well aware of the underlying threat in the

statement. It was he, if he should win, who would be largely responsible for mainland reprisals against the Islands.

He sat there listening to Darrow, the man whose concept of justice was so different from his own. The thought may very well have occurred to him that it would not be too difficult, even now, to accept Darrow's view of justice. It was not so wrong as it was different. Go along with it and Admiral Stirling would honor him; the kamaaina elite here, the millions on the mainland, the watchful powers in Washington, would praise the magnificent gesture.

He could never hope to match Darrow's eloquence. It might be better for the Islands if he didn't even try.

Darrow had again brought him into the picture.

"I know the state's attorney would rather convict four people instead of two, but I think he would compromise on two. That ought to be enough for one day."

He was referring to the two seamen.

"If you needed a friend would you take one of these gobs, or would you wait outside prayer meetings on Wednesday night—I guess that's the right night? I say to you that I would take one of these, rather than the others.

"Tommy had prepared this warrant or subpoena, woven, like Joseph's coat, of many colors. Jones handed it to the Hawaiian boy and said Major Ross wanted to see him. They did not want to kill. They made no plan to kill. They didn't know what to do when it happened. And the house was not a good place to kill . . . one family thirty feet away, another house twenty-five feet away." Irony underscored his words as he flung a look at Kelley. "A lovely place to kill someone, isn't it?"

This was the rational basis of his plea—the powerful logic, the common-sense view which was always interwoven with the warp of feeling

He went on tirelessly: "I haven't always had the highest opinion of the average human being; man is none too great at best. He is moved by everything that reaches him, but I have no reason to think there is anybody on this jury who will disregard the truth for some fantastic, imaginary theory. Tommy had told you the fact that there was no intention of killing. When Kahahawai said, 'Yes—I done it,' everything was blotted out. Here was the man who had ruined his wife!"

Then, with ringing solemnity, reminding the jury of the awful burden of responsibility which was theirs, he said: "No man can judge another unless he places himself in the position of the other before he pronounces the verdict.

"If you put yourself in Tommy Massie's place, what would you have done?" His eyes made a searching probe of each member of the jury: "I don't know about you, or you, or you . . . but at least ten out of twelve men would have done just what poor Tommy Massie did.

"Massie saw the picture of his wife pleading, injured, raped . . . and he shot! And then what? Had any preparations been made to get out this body? What could they do? What would you have done with a dead man on your hands? You would want to protect yourselves. It might be the wrong thing to do . . . but it's only human.

"What is the first instinct? Flight! To the mountains, to the sea, anywhere but where they were. Here was the dead body. They couldn't leave it. Perhaps they could get rid of it. There isn't one in ten thousand who wouldn't get away, no matter how."

He let that sink in, then, with a sorrowful shake of the head: "That isn't the plan of conduct of someone who had thought out a definite plan; it is the hasty, half-coordinated instinct of one surprised in a situation. And finally they were caught."

This was Darrow's American tragedy, his fight for those who hadn't been able to get away with it, who deserved, now that they had been caught, that he give them his best.

His best included a shrewd if none-too-hopeful reminder of Tommy's "black-out."

"Gradually, Lieutenant Massie was coming back to consciousness and realizing where he was. Where is the mystery in a man cracking up after six or eight months of worry?"

He concentrated his attention on the non-Haole members of the jury.

"I have looked at this Island, which is a new country to me. I've never had any prejudice against any race on earth. I didn't learn it, and I defy anyone to find any word of mine to contradict what I say. To me these questions of race must be solved by understanding—not by force."

He was coming now to his peroration. With only a brief respite, he had spoken now for more than four hours. He was tired. As the poet had said of him, there was pathos now in his face and in his eyes, and weariness.

"I have put this case without appeal to the nationality or race of any juror, asking them to pass on it as a human case.

"We're all human beings. Take this case with its dire disasters, written all over by the hand of fate, as a case of your own, and I'll be content with your verdict."

Uncompromising determinist that he was, passionately convinced that environment not heredity made the man, he said: "What we do is affected by things around us; we're made more than we make.

"I want you to help this family, to understand them. If you understand them, that's all that's necessary. I'd like to think I had done my small part to bring peace and justice to an Island wracked and worn by strife. You have not only the fate but the life of these four people. What is there for them if you pronounce a sentence of doom on them? What have they done?

"You are a people to heal, not to destroy. I place this in your hands asking you to be kind and considerate both to the living and the dead."

His eyes had filled with tears. His words had brought tears to many in the courtroom. He turned and sank into his chair. It was not the first time his plea for suffering humanity had made him cry. The atheist had made his own peace with himself, by assuming the mantle of a savior.

Much of what he had said was already being broadcast to the mainland. It would continue even while Kelley made his closing speech for the state.

TWENTY-FOUR

"You have been presented with an argument of passion, not reason, a plea of sympathy, not insanity!"

The words lunged straight at the heart of Darrow's defense.

Whether or not Kelley had wondered about the advisability of softening his attack, it was electrifyingly clear now that it was no longer a temptation. Darrow's eloquence was not going to confuse the issue. Kelley was out to win. He stood foursquare for the law. He was against those who violated it. The jury must "judge on facts and law!" The rest was blarney!

He stood, a massive, immovable bulwark against "consideration and sympathy." The overt hostility of the Haoles in the courtroom served only as a spur. To them he was the assassin of all they held dear. He was a traitor to his own kind, already an outcast.

His voice steeled itself against their hatred. For Tommy, he had nothing but contempt.

"I could point out the selfishness of this man who took his wife to a dance against her will. He says his wife doesn't like these parties and has walked away from others."

Scornfully he cried: "I could point out to you the evasions in Massie's account of the night at the Inn, yet Darrow says he is frank!"

Now he showed his fiery reaction to the introduction of expert testimony. "Fifty years ago no one heard of a defense of temporary insanity. Now it is used by moneyed parties to hide behind conveniently. Convenient insanity . . . from the time of the Harry Thaw case to now!

"Thalia Massie was at the party against her will, and left the party disgusted through the fault of her husband. His action is the basis for all these events and for the death of Kahahawai!

"They put that girl on the stand for no other purpose than to excite your sympathy—" He swung his bulky but athletically managed frame to glare at the fashionably dressed white woman in the first row of the public section. "—and that of the clique whose disgraceful demonstration was so severely reprimanded by the Court!"

It was not the clique he was excoriating, so much as the power of the *kamaaina* elite which their presence represented.

"They took him [Kahahawai] on an unlawful, felonious expedition. They admit it. They used a gun on him. You don't have to believe that they intended to kill him."

But was not his death, he pointed out, the natural and probable consequence of their act?

Too well did Kelley know that he lacked Darrow's oratorical gifts. Righteous indignation was his weapon against them. Powerful recognition of the rights of the dead man.

"Are you going to follow the law of Hawaii, or the argument of Darrow? The same presumption of innocence that clothes these defendants, clothed Kahahawai and went down with him to his grave. He went to his grave, in the eyes of the law, an innocent man, regardless of what any of us may think. They have removed by their act the possibility of his ever being other than an innocent man, regardless of whether or not the other Ala Moana defendants are found guilty."

He stared deliberately at Tommy. Lips tightly compressed, his eyes expressionless, Tommy stared beyond Kelley toward the open window of the courtroom. There was sky and green hills—the verdant crater of the Punchbowl. *Ewa* was Pearl Harbor, the submarine base. Perhaps he remembered something that Darrow had said of him. "The only safe place for Massie was in a submarine." In this underwater womb there was safety. Men without women. He had made a mess of the rest—bungled it.

He was beyond caring what Kelley would say about him. It had all been said.

But Kelley had plenty to say to those who listened.

"Do any of you doubt that Lieutenant Massie was tight at the party, that his officer friend was drunk? The most you can say for Massie is that he lied like a gentleman. We brought on all the evidence we had. Did they?" He shook his head. "Lieutenant Massie has been the oracle for all that happened at the Fortescue house . . ."

He stared at the other defendants who could have been oracles if Darrow had wanted it.

"They aren't kids. They're brought up in an atmosphere of guns . . . three able men . . . and a cold, calculating woman!"

The description did not shock Mrs. Fortescue. Nothing that the prosecution had to say would surprise her.

Kelley went on: "They're taught the art of killing, also of first aid. But they let him die, dragged him into the bathroom like a dog and let him die.

"If Kahahawai had said 'Yes—we done it' . . . which a Hawaiian would *not* say, even an ignorant Hawaiian . . . did you ever hear of a dying statement by a man about to face his Maker with this burden?

"But these people told of no such statement."

He could not resist a riposte to Darrow's attacks on him. "I expected that in their defense by these high-powered attorneys, we would be told that as he lay dying, he told what had happened."

Now he picked up Tommy's own gun, the weapon which had lain concealed behind a cushion of the chaise. It lay snug in the fleshy palm of his hand.

"Lieutenant Massie, if he had taken this gun and mowed these men down in the hospital when his wife identified them, he'd at least have had the respect of the community, however wrong in law that act might have been." Again there was the deprecating shake of the head. "He waited months and dragged in these enlisted men. But they were free and voluntary parties to the act, and are therefore fully responsible. A killing is a killing, and under certain circumstances is murder!"

Darrow sat heavily in his chair, arms on the table, head bowed.

"In the Loeb-Leopold case—"

Darrow's head came up.

"—Darrow said he hated killing, regardless of how it was done, always had and always will. And now he comes before you and says a killing is justified and is not murder."

Darrow bowed his head once more.

Now Kelley pounded home what he believed was really at issue here.

"Hawaii is on trial! Is there to be one law for strangers and another for us? Are strangers to come here and take the law in their own hands? Are you going to give Lieutenant Massie leave to walk out?

"They'll make him an admiral!" he exploded. "They'll make him Chief of Staff! He and Admiral Pratt are of the same mind. They believe in lynch law!"

He aimed a finger at the flag. "As long as the American flag flies on that staff—without an Admiral's pennant over it, you must regard the constitution and the law. You have taken an oath to uphold it . . ." The pointed finger swung to Tommy. ". . . and he is here because he violated that oath."

He turned to the jury once more.

"Do your duty uninfluenced by influence of sympathy, by influence of admirals." Admirals were an opportunity for the Irish rebel that was in him. "As Smedley Butler said, 'To hell with the admirals!'"

"Our navy—under fire without reason!" cried the press that same day.

Kelley took it in stride.

What remained now was for Judge Davis to instruct the jury, to reread the indictment to them, to point out to the panel the distinction between murder in the first degree and murder in the second, and to explain how these differed from manslaughter, which was also a possible verdict.

TWENTY-FIVE

By the afternoon of the following day, when no news had come from the jury room, or as Admiral Stirling put it, "the six white men on the jury were yet fighting for white men's justice," the word "deadlock" began to be heard among the throngs which throughout the trial had clogged the streets surrounding the Judiciary Building, and had turned the Iolani Palace grounds into their whispering gallery.

The defendants had been lodged overnight in a nearby hotel. With them was Captain Wortman, commander of the submarine base and Tommy's superior officer, who as a temporary deputy of the court was responsible for them.

No one cared to express an opinion on the outcome, least of all Darrow. He had in fact been invited to a garden party at Admiral Stirling's quarters, where the Admiral was entertaining the officers of a foreign warship. There was a whisper, which Darrow preferred to disregard, that in the event of conviction, Governor Judd would issue pardons at once.

Admiral Stirling did not like the significance of what lay behind that whisper. Was this something that had come down from Washington? If so, why was it necessary? Surely the possibility of a guilty verdict was out of the question! There was only one possible verdict—acquittal—unless of course, the white men on the jury were being forced "to bow to the dictates of the orientals."

It was inconceivable. Yet it might very well happen. The Admiral could only hope, in a remarkable gesture of resignation to Island realities, that the Governor could be relied upon to keep his word.

The presence of these so-called orientals on the jury—only two of whom could actually be described as being oriental—was as disturbing to Mrs. Fortescue as it was to the Admiral.

She had wondered all along, and still did, how Darrow's wisdom, his brilliant advocacy of the true morality, could penetrate to the minds of six men to whom the white man's code was a mystery. It was no part of her wonder that the articles of that code were not particularly clear-cut. It was better to wonder and deplore oriental backwardness than to examine the code. ·

When twenty-four hours had passed and there was still no word from the jury, guessing games in the whispering gallery produced the hopeful rumor that the jury now stood ten to two for acquittal.

It could not be long now.

Kelley's office was being inundated with letters and cablegrams from the mainland. Very few were complimentary.

He should be "hung" from a lamppost and a fire set under it . . .

He was a disgrace to the good old Irish name of Kelley . . .

He was a disgrace to American manhood . . .

How could a man with a white skin so far forget himself as to persecute his own?

Fearing violence, as well as the possibility that the jury room might have been bugged, court officers searched the room periodically. The number of men guarding the entrances to the Judiciary Building was increased. Police cars armed with tear gas, shotguns and submachine guns patrolled the area.

By the following day, when it was rumored that the number of ballots taken by the jury had now reached twenty-two, it was being said that Judge Davis was discussing with counsel, the advisability of "sandbagging" the jury. Darrow objected. He wanted no pressure put on the panel.

At five-thirty that afternoon, forty-nine hours after their deliberations had begun, the jury sent word to the judge that they had reached a verdict.

The principals were summoned to the courtroom.

Police lined the entrance and kept the lobby clear as judge and jury waited for the defendants to arrive.

Mrs. Fortescue was the first. She was accompanied by her brother, Robert Bell, and her sister, Mrs. Helen Ripley, both of whom had come from the mainland to be at her side. They moved stiffly past the guards, strangely disconnected from their surroundings. They were like foreign passengers in transit through an exotic, bewildering and frightening land, giving nothing of themselves to the incomprehensible society in which they were trapped.

They were followed into the building by Tommy and Thalia. Lord and Jones were behind them. A policeman ordered Lord to get rid of his cigaret. He snapped it away with a smile more uncertain than defiant.

The jury filed into the courtroom when defendants and counsel were all present. Admiral Stirling, hastening to court from the naval base, had not yet arrived. The Judge did not wait.

"Gentlemen of the jury, have you reached a verdict?"

Habituation had not blunted the terrifying quality of the question, nor the fateful nature of the reply, "Yes, your Honor."

The Judge had ordered the defendants to rise. Thalia, rising with Tommy, had to be reminded by a bailiff that she was not a defendant.

"But he's my husband!"

Tommy nudged her. She sat down.

The foreman of the jury, a white man, handed the verdicts, written on four separate sheets of paper, to the clerk, who in turn handed them to the Judge. No one could tell, as they looked toward the Judge, what he read. That was to come, when he returned the verdicts to the clerk, to be read aloud.

"We, the jury, find the defendant, Thomas H. Massie, guilty of manslaughter, and recommend leniency."

At once there was a gasping sob of disbelief by Thalia. She began to cry. Tommy touched her shoulder. She bowed her head, weeping silently as the three remaining verdicts were read, all, save for the names, finding the same verdict, finding them all guilty of manslaughter and recommending leniency. Interior shock lay revealed in the fixed stare of

Mrs. Fortescue's eyes. Tommy's eyes were sad. The seamen stood impassively at attention. The brother and sister of Mrs. Fortescue sat unchanged.

Save for Thalia, it was Darrow who seemed most affected. His mouth worked, but he said nothing, maintaining his silence until the Judge had dismissed the jury. Had he hoped to make of this case a fitting climax to his long career? The unexpected and disastrous shock of disappointment was clear to see, yet he was able to rebound aggressively.

"This fight has just begun!"

Admiral Stirling, arriving too late to hear the verdict, did not have to be told that it had gone against them.

It could only be the Governor's doing! It was his "fine Italian hand" which had insinuated itself into the case, promising a pardon in order to get a conviction. Now, master of intrigue that he was, he would probably go back on that promise!

The truth was that there was no intrigue by the Governor. The jury judged the case purely on its merits. One member was to say later that Darrow spoke to them like a bunch of farmers.

An "oriental" member of the jury, Theodore Char, a Honolulu accountant who had attended the universities of Illinois and Chicago, put it this way:

"The jury in the case was guided solely by the evidence and by the fact that law and order must prevail in the Hawaiian Islands. There were no racial lines in our deliberations . . .

"We all appreciated the suffering caused Lieutenant Massie and Mrs. Fortescue by the assault . . . but we all agreed that no amount of suffering caused one man by another could be legal justification for taking that man's life . . .

"We came to the conclusion that Massie was sane when the killing took place . . . Some jurors believed that he was evasive at many points. Many of us thought that if the defense were sincere they would have put Mrs. Fortescue, Lord and Jones, on the stand. I, for one, would have liked to hear their stories.

"Mrs. Massie created a very favorable and sympathetic

feeling when she testified about the assault and told of her suffering. We all felt sorry for her. But none of us approved her action in snatching the paper from Prosecutor Kelley's hands and tearing it up . . . I think this somewhat influenced some of the jurors, including white men, against her and tended to discredit her testimony . . .

"We recommended leniency in our verdict because none of us wanted to see the defendants punished too severely after what they had already gone through."

The Judge, announcing that sentence would be deferred for a week, agreed to allow the defendants to return to the station ship *Alton* provided the order permitting this was still in effect.

Kelley, made overconfident by the verdict, doubted whether such an order had ever existed officially, and said so. Captain Wortman turned on him in a fury: "You know dawn well there is!"

"I do not!"

Wortman eyed him bitterly: "You know damn little!"

The Judge confirmed the existence of the order.

Unexpectedly, Tommy offered Kelley his hand. "If I ever had anything against you, Mr. Kelley—"

Kelley did not allow him to finish. He took Tommy's hand. "I haven't anything against you personally . . . nor against your wife."

Instantly, Thalia shot back: "Oh no! You haven't anything against me!"

She might have gone on—perhaps even to slap him—had not Tommy restrained her. "Now Thalia—" he chided her, like the patient, long-suffering guardian of a willful child.

"I expected it!" Mrs. Fortescue snapped at a reporter, as she was leaving the building. Her voice icy with disdain, bitterly revolted, she said: "I felt all along that we would be unable to get a fair and just trial in Honolulu. American womanhood means nothing, even to white people in Honolulu."

But Tommy resigned himself gallantly to Hawaiian justice.

"If I have done wrong, I am not afraid of punishment."

They were the words of a man who seemed to prefer to deny himself the natural human instinct for survival, one whose resignation utterly negated all Darrow's work.

But this kind of martyrdom was hardly acceptable to mainland defenders of American womanhood and white supremacy. The hurricane winds of their displeasure with the verdict blew into Washington next morning. Washington funneled the storm directly back at Hawaii.

TWENTY-SIX

After a night's sleep, Darrow was sufficiently recovered from the disastrous blow to his confidence to loose a furious volley at Hawaiian justice.

"The verdict is a travesty!"

He followed it up with a barrage of denunciatory fire which brought immediate and enthusiastic approval from the mainland.

"It was a travesty on justice and human nature!" he thundered, "—on every emotion that has made us what we are from the day the human race was born!"

Now he zeroed in on the jury itself.

"It doesn't seem possible that intelligent-looking, kindly men could wish to make the defendants' burden greater and add to the terrible picture of their wrongs. The jurors were in a position to heal up and bind the wounds and bring love and happiness and understanding, but they saw fit to convict!"

He was putting Hawaii on notice that the verdict was totally unacceptable to him. It could not be allowed to stand.

"It may take three or four years before the outcome of this case is decided. I intend to stick to it to the very end!"

He could not understand, he said, why the four defendants were convicted for something that Lieutenant Massie never intended to do.

He could only attribute it to the fact that ". . . the greater part of the jury had closed their minds to any thought but conviction. When I gazed into those dark faces, I could see the deep mysteries of the Orient were there. My ideas and words were not registering."

This was strange talk coming from the lips of a man who had said to the jury in his closing speech, "I've never had any prejudice against any race on earth. I didn't learn it, and I defy anyone to find any word of mine to contradict what I say."

Darrow's fulminations at Hawaiian justice had hardly been broadcast to the mainland when there began to appear in every edition of the Hearst newspaper chain, a front page-box which importuned readers to:

URGE SOLONS TO DEMAND ACTION IN HAWAII!

Write Your Representatives in Washington to Take the Necessary Steps to Protect the Honor of American Womanhood in the American Possession of Hawaii, and Also to Compel Decent Respect on the Part of the Hawaiian Rabble for Our American Nation and Our Nation's Patriotic Defenders!

Letters, wires, telephone calls, flooded a capital already described as stunned by the verdict.

When it was learned that President Hoover did not have the power to issue pardons in the Territory of Hawaii any more than he had in the states, Senator J. Hamilton Lewis of Illinois asserted that the President did have that power and should exercise it immediately.

Dudley Field Malone, eminent attorney and close friend of Darrow's, who had, for a time, considered joining the latter as his associate in the trial, now voiced the feelings of many in a telegram to President Hoover in which he urged the President to do now what he should have done at the beginning:

Order Lieutenant Massie, his wife, his mother-in-law and the two enlisted men on board a warship and bring them to the first port of jurisdiction on the mainland, namely San Francisco, where they can get a fair trial and the protection American citizens should be properly entitled to!

Congress took up the cry. Senator McKellar of Tennessee was convinced that the trial had been unfair. "Local prejudice evidently controlled it."

Senator Robinson of Indiana expressed his horror at this deplorable let-down in the standards of justice. Had he been on the jury, he declared, he would have freed the defendants.

"Something's wrong in Hawaii," cried Senator Copeland, "when so cruel a verdict can be rendered in an American possession. No wonder the telegraph is hot with protests this morning!"

Senator King of Utah, reluctant though he was to criticize courts and juries, could not help but feel that the verdict was a miscarriage of justice.

More threatening was the opinion of the ranking Republican on the House Naval Affairs Committee, Fred A. Britten of Illinois, whose consternation at the verdict led directly to a stern demand for immediate reprisals.

"I believe the duty of our Government now," Britten announced, "is to see that law and order are maintained in Hawaii, even if it becomes necessary to establish some form of military rule." Reinforcing the viewpoint of Admiral Stirling, he added: "Hawaii is too important to us from a defense viewpoint not to be governed properly."

Floyd Gibbons, the internationally known war correspondent, seconded this proposal for his millions of readers in his characteristically breezy but big-stick style:

Hello everybody! Here's news . . . good news!

It comes hot off the floor of the American Publishers' Association convention just closing in New York this week . . . I didn't expect attention would be attracted and interest aroused so spontaneously at a period when other subjects of vital importance hold the public spotlight. But the comic opera mismanagement of America's Pacific Gibraltar has done just that, and I think I know the reason.

It is that a national danger is sensed. Political control of Uncle Sam's most important defense in the Pacific has been allowed to pass into the hands of Asiatic politicians, or politicians whose utterances and policies are based on a desire to cultivate and attract the support and advantage of the over-whelmingly Asiatic majority of the population. This fact has at last been brought home to us just as though we had suddenly found there was a leak in the boat and immediate danger of sinking . . .

America's reply should be:

Don't give up the ship!

Don't give up the white women in Hawaii!

Don't give up the Hawaiian Islands to Asiatic politicians!

Hawaii is an American outpost!

It might well be the Sumpter [sic!] of the next war!

It should be governed by the Army or Navy of the United States in the interest and for the protection of the American nation!

Although Hawaii did indeed become the Sumter of the next war, the "Asiatics" whom Gibbons feared formed the volunteer 442nd Regimental Combat Team in Hawaii which won glory at Salerno and Anzio, and courageously rescued the Texan "Lost Battalion" in Southern France . . .

Beset though he was by domestic woes, by the seemingly insoluble problem of mass unemployment at home, President Hoover, while saying nothing for publication, could not help but be affected by the torrent of appeals and protests which invaded the White House. The powerful and influential Navy League demanded of him that he do something to punish Hawaii.

Hawaii's Delegate to Congress, Victor S. K. Houston, alarmed by pressure which had built up to the point where enabling legislation to impose commission rule on Hawaii was being hurriedly drafted, cabled his fears to Governor Judd. With his cable went a petition signed by twenty-nine members of Congress, pleading for the freeing of the defendants.

As President Hoover's appointee, the Governor realized that he was not free to exercise independent judgment. Some means of appeasing the mainland would have to be worked out.

Forty-eight hours before the date set for sentencing, the Navy cars which had transported the defendants each day during the trial drew up unexpectedly before the Judiciary Building.

From one of the cars stepped Tommy, Thalia and Mrs. Fortescue. From the other came the seamen Jones and Lord. The five were swiftly escorted into the building by Captain Wortman and an aide, their arrival going almost unnoticed.

There were only a few of the perennial courtroom habitués present when they entered. Certainly those few did not expect to be favored with a glimpse of the defendants in the Massie case.

The defendants occupied the same seats in the courtroom in which they had been seated during the trial and from which they had risen to hear the verdict.

A minute or two after ten o'clock, Darrow and Kelley came from the Judge's chambers and took their accustomed places in court. Their associates were already present.

All rose as Judge Davis entered the courtroom.

Now Prosecutor Kelley, his face set, his voice cold and harsh, rose to make the motion that sentencing of the defendants take place forthwith.

The defendants stood up. So did Darrow. They stood there facing the bench in the classic tableau of the People versus the Accused, prepared to hear the punishment which the Court saw fit to levy on them for their crime.

Did Lieutenant Massie have anything to say before sentence was passed upon him?

He murmured, "No, your Honor."

The question was repeated to Mrs. Fortescue, to Jones, to Lord.

None had anything to say.

Beginning now with one of the seamen, the Judge read the sentence:

"In accordance with the verdict of manslaughter returned against you in this case, I hereby sentence you to the term prescribed by law, not more than ten years' imprisonment at hard labor at Oahu Prison."

Jones showed no sign of emotion.

In solemn, magisterial cadence, the Judge repeated the sentence for each of the defendants. Each, in turn, accepted the punishment as Jones had.

Now, in accordance with the ritual which would, for ten years, deprive the defendants of their freedom, and put them to hard labor, Kelley, as harshly as before, moved for a writ of mittimus, the implacable step which would transfer the defendants to their warders.

Only then did the charade-like nature of this procedure, this masquerade of justice and courtroom solemnity dissolve into its latent purpose.

"Before the writ is issued," said the Judge, "I want the bailiffs to clear the courtroom of all except counsel and the defendants."

The masquerade was to be a private affair. The Judge wanted no witnesses to what was perhaps the real travesty.

The High Sheriff of the City and County of Hawaii now entered the Courtroom. He was Major Ross, the same Ross whose name Mrs. Fortescue had chosen to lend authority to the forged document which had lured Kahahawai to his death. He had not come to sue for the misuse of his name but to accept the writ of mittimus which would deliver up the prisoners to him.

A half-smile of cynical resignation played about Kelley's lips as he watched the defendants file from the courtroom, followed by the slow-moving Darrow. He folded his arms in a final gesture of objection to what he knew was to come.

Escorted by Major Ross, Darrow and the defendants looked for all the world like tourists in the company of their guide. Here on the Iolani Palace grounds was where the annual parade in honor of King Kamehameha would begin in a few weeks. Over there was the old Fort, the Library of Hawaii, the Kawaiahao Church. And just beyond the banyans there, is the Palace itself. It was the high point of their tour. They were invited to enter.

The royal dining hall of Hawaii's Kings and Queens, the royal apartment where Queen Liliuokalani spent a desolate year as a prisoner of the Hawaiian Republic which had deposed her, and now the lofty, red-carpeted chamber of the Governor.

It had all been rehearsed, secretly planned in all its detail during the two days prior to this visit.

First the Shakespearean chorus to this masque—the actor, Clarence Darrow, reading from a scroll.

"The undersigned defendants," he intoned, "defendants in the matter of the Territory of Hawaii versus Grace Fortescue et al, and their attorneys, do hereby respectfully pray that your Excellency, in the exercise of the power of executive clemency in you vested, and further in view of the recommendation of the jury in said matter, do commute the sentences heretofore pronounced in said matter!"

The play had begun! The actors were on their marks. The Governor at his desk, the petitioners before him, their attorney in fatherly position beside them. The Governor studied the petition, as rehearsed. He thought about it, as rehearsed. A moment or two of suspenseful hesitancy, also as rehearsed.

Was there any doubt about whether he would grant the petition, whether it was fitting that it should be granted? If so, it was only in the Governor's mind, for now, eying the petitioners benevolently he said that he would indeed commute their sentences—to one hour!

That hour, as it happened, was already up. It was time to celebrate. Newspapermen and photographers were invited into the Governor's office. There should have been champagne. Thalia was radiant. Tommy, flinging an arm around Darrow for the benefit of the photographers, hailed him as the greatest man in the world. No one reminded him of the martyred air with which he had been prepared to accept punishment. Nor did anyone suggest that more powerful forces than Darrow might have been instrumental in getting him his freedom.

Not that the commutation was real freedom, as a petition bearing the names of 1100 Haole members of Honolulu's Citizens' Organization for Good Government stated that very day. The petition pleaded with the Governor to substitute full pardons for commutation. It was followed next day by a congressional petition signed by 107 members of Congress, also asking for a full pardon. A bill, introduced by Senator Logan of Kentucky, empowered the President to pardon any defendant convicted in a Territorial court of a criminal offense. The bill was not passed, nor the full pardons granted.

Now, when she could speak freely, when there was opportunity to give vent to all her anger and bitterness and outrage, Mrs. Fortescue could only cry, "When I leave here I never want to come back as long as I live!"

Kelley, as Public Prosecutor, now prepared for the retrial of the four defendants in the Ala Moana case. Lightning switch though it was, he would surely be as conscientious in prosecuting the case as he had been in the Massie case. One may doubt however whether he hoped or even wanted to win.

Darrow however, wanted him to dismiss the case. He had no desire to subject Thalia to the ordeal of telling again the sordid details of that crime. It would be useless, he said, to waste time and money on it. Since the jury had disagreed once, he would be satisfied if the entire matter was dropped, even though Thalia had told him that she wanted to stay for the retrial. It would be rather absurd, he said, for Kelley, who had prosecuted her mother and husband in the Kahahawai trial to turn around and be on her side against the four remaining defendants in the Ala Moana case.

Kelley did not think it was absurd at all. He believed that out of respect to herself, her family and her country, Thalia should stay to face the ordeal, however painful. He seemed almost too eager to have her stay. The prosecutor was behaving suspiciously like a defender.

It was a role which he was to be denied, for five days later, Thalia, together with Tommy and Mrs. Fortescue, as well as Darrow, sailed for San Francisco, evading the process-servers who attempted to go aboard to serve her with a subpoena to appear at the retrial.

Lord and Jones had left quietly two or three days earlier. They had been assured, as was Tommy, that in the eyes of the Navy, their conviction of a felony was without merit. "Naval authorities," said Admiral Stirling, "tacitly have refused to consider legal either the trial or the conviction."

TWENTY-SEVEN

Without Thalia present to testify against the four remaining defendants in the Ala Moana case, the charges against them were dropped. They were free.

Urged by the San Francisco press upon her arrival in that city, Thalia had written an innocent and touching account of her part in the affair, which began: "It was with strangely-mixed emotions that I looked through a porthole on the steamer 'Malolo' and watched the island of Oahu, Hawaii, fade into nothingness the other day . . ."

The story changed nothing that she had said in her testimony. The defendants were guilty. Her identification of them was true. The defense attorneys were unethical. She had not stayed for the retrial to be further humiliated and degraded. She was glad it was over.

It was not over for Governor Judd. Troubled and uncertain, made the whipping boy for mainland anger, he now decided to engage Pinkerton's National Detective Agency to make a thorough investigation of the Ala Moana affair. He chose Pinkerton's only because the FBI did not operate in the Islands.

Early in June, experienced operatives of the detective agency began a systematic and exhaustive check of all who had been involved in the case.

Their investigation continued throughout the summer. No possible source of information or enlightenment was left unexamined. They questioned police officers and government officials, doctors, Navy officers and their wives, the four surviving defendants and their relatives, the witnesses who had testified for and against them and even some who had never been called. Their investigations took them as far afield as Bayport, Long Island, and Washington, D. C.

It was in questioning police officers and emergency hospital personnel, that it soon began to be apparent to the investigators that the more opportunity Thalia had been given to see the defendants, the more details she remembered about them. Yet the record showed indisputably that prior to having them brought before her she could furnish absolutely no description of her assailants to the police. On the basis of this immediate discovery, it seemed justifiable to the Pinkerton men to doubt the accuracy of the personal identifications which she made later.

Soon also, they discovered that the license number of the Ida car had been broadcast repeatedly within earshot of both Thalia and Tommy when Thalia was being examined at the Emergency Hospital. According to one police officer who was present, officer friends of Tommy who were with him at the hospital showed a great deal of interest in that license number when they kept hearing it repeated.

Did they make sure that Thalia had also heard it? The investigators did not know.

The investigation of the rape itself was of course their prime objective.

Thalia had testified to being raped four to six times by five men, and had been badly beaten by them. There were certain factors connected with rape which the Pinkerton men deemed it vital to consider.

In a gang rape of this nature, they believed, it was improbable that any consideration whatsoever would be shown to the victim, or any care of her would be taken by these men while raping her. Thalia had testified that one of the men savagely struck her in the jaw while he was raping her. They were all young and athletic and naturally would have hurried and been violent in their behavior.

Yet, although Thalia had testified that her assailants had dragged her along the ground, the investigators discovered that the shoes she wore that night showed no signs of such treatment. As to the rest of her clothes, a careful examination by laboratory personnel failed to show any evidence of an attack such as she described, the garments being in perfect condition, no rips or tears, except on one stocking.

To the investigators it seemed improbable that an attack such as Thalia described would not show some evidence on clothing of such flimsy material. Even had her clothing been turned up above the hips, to quote the Pinkerton men, there would certainly be indications of some nature caused by the character of the ground on which she lay.

The doctor at the Emergency Hospital who had examined her about two and a half hours after the alleged rape, examined the vaginal area and found no abrasions or contusions.

The Navy doctor who examined her later that day made no mention of vaginal injuries in his testimony at the rape trial.

The laboratory physician who had examined scrapings following her curettement, stated in his report that there was no evidence of pregnancy.

The laboratory chief at Queens Hospital examined both the slip and step-ins which she had worn, and found no evidence of sperm.

In examining the five defendants approximately thirty-six hours after the assault, an Emergency Hospital doctor said that he found no evidence of traumatism, blood or genital secretions, nor was there any sperm on their clothing, although it was the same which they had worn on the night of the attack.

In their report to the Governor—not delivered to him until the following October—Pinkerton's stated:

We have found nothing in the record of this case, nor have we through our own efforts been able to find, what in our estimation would be sufficient corroboration of the statements of Mrs. Massie to establish the occurrence of rape upon her. There is a preponderance of evidence that Mrs. Massie did in some manner suffer numerous bruises about the head and body, but definite proof of actual rape has not in our opinion been found.

The investigators devoted considerable time to checking and rechecking the conflicting times of arrivals and departures.

Based on the assumption that Thalia had left the Ala Wai Inn at about midnight, it seemed to them that—

in view of the evidence as to the movements and the time of the accused from eleven-thirty p.m. until twelve-thirty-seven a.m. [the time at which the Ida car had been in near-collision with the Peeples' car], there was not opportunity for the accused to commit the kidnapping and the rape of Mrs. Massie, either at the time alleged by her, or at other times within this period. For such to have been possible, it would be necessary for many witnesses to have wilfully made false statements and to have perjured themselves at the trial of the accused.

Even if Thalia had left the Inn at 11:35 P.M. instead of at midnight, as she testified at the trial, she would have been at the point where she was kidnapped at 11:45 P.M. She and the defendants would have arrived at the old quarantine grounds at 11:49. Then, allowing twenty minutes for the rape, she would have reappeared on the Ala Moana boulevard, where she was seen by the Bellingers and the Clarks, at 12:16 A.M.

The fact was, however, that she did not hail the Bellinger car until approximately 12:50 P.M.

In other words, there is a period of some forty minutes when her whereabouts remained wrapped in mystery.

The concluding passage of the Pinkerton Report could not have been more level-headed and impartial:

It seems fair to assume, it stated, "that the prosecution of the accused was forced upon the Territory by reason of Mrs. Massie's story and her identification of these boys. No other course appears to have been possible in view of the circumstances, than to try the case which had its basis and support exclusively upon Mrs. Massie's narrative and identifications.

That the prosecution failed for want of corroboration of essential parts of Mrs. Massie's story, . . . was inevitable.

Thus, the question of who had actually beaten her remained unanswered. Whether or not she had actually been raped . . . that too remained open to question . . .

Its existence known to only a few, for it was never made public, the Pinkerton Report lies on a shelf in a vault of Hawaii's Archives Building.

TWENTY-EIGHT

While it seemed abundantly clear that the Pinkerton Report had virtually established the innocence of the defendants in the Ala Moana case, it is surprising that Governor Judd was to express his disappointment with it by saying that the report had shed no new light on the situation. One cannot help wondering what further illumination he had hoped for. At any rate, he decided not to make the report public, because, as he himself said, it would only have stirred up more trouble. Thirty-five years later he still maintained that this was his reason for withholding its release.

If he saw his decision as a commendable stand, born perhaps of some mistaken urge to let Hawaii suffer the onslaughts of mainland anger, his secrecy served only to crystallize mainland attitudes and produce the very trouble which he feared.

Earlier, in reflecting the dismay of the non-Haole community with the commutation of the sentences in the Massie case, Princess Kawakanakoa, one of the few remaining Hawaiians of royal blood, who was also a Republican National Committeewoman, had angrily asked: "Are we to infer from the Governor's act that there are two sets of laws in Hawaii—one for the favored few, and another for the people in general?"

Now, unaware of the Pinkerton Report findings or of the Governor's reasons for not making them public, she was to have her question answered directly from Washington.

Hard on the heels of the Governor's decision to withhold the document, and soon after the election of President Franklin D. Roosevelt, a bill was introduced in Congress, by Senator Hiram Bingham of Connecticut, which called for putting Hawaii under the jurisdiction of the Navy Department. Fulfilling the desires of Admiral Stirling, the bill also provided for the Territory to be ruled by a commission form of government.

Whether it was because of a sudden uncertainty about the righteousness of their cause, or because they felt that the devil they knew was better than the devil they did not know, the very Haoles who had cried the loudest for reform, who had pressed the hardest for at least a decade of military government, now shrank from the prospect of Navy jurisdiction.

All at once, these xenophobic members of the *kamaiiana* elite developed a praiseworthy tolerance of Island justice, as well as of the existence of too many non-Haole legislators. Their tolerance may even have extended to the Massie case. Perhaps the verdict had been just, after all! Was there also a remote likelihood that the guilt of the defendants in the Ala Moana case had indeed been in doubt?

Forthwith, Walter Dillingham, one of the leaders of the *kamaiiana* elite, instructed his agent in Washington to persuade Senator Bingham to withdraw the bill. The bill was never passed. Paradoxically, Haole opposition to its passage began to have the inadvertent effect of imposing a curb on mainland hostility. There was even a dawning of respect for non-Haoles as Hawaiian citizens. They were no longer regarded as merely the irresponsible and dangerous wards of the mainland. It was as though the Massie case, in the very rage and violence which it provoked, had held up a mirror fleetingly to the illogic and savagery of Haole and mainland reaction, giving them all reason to pause.

But more trouble was to come! The reflection in the mirror had not been seen by all. That same year, a bill was introduced by Representative John E. Rankin of Mississippi, and supported by President Roosevelt, which would have permitted the President to appoint a mainlander as Governor of the Islands.

Again, the *kamaiiana* elite protested. They did not want

a mainlander, civilian or military, to run Hawaii. Again, Congress paused. On the mainland it began to be felt that Haole-non-Haole antagonism was a kind of family fight in which it was best not to interfere. The measure was never enacted.

This was a second disappointment for Admiral Stirling, who now inveighed darkly against the Islands by warning its citizens that henceforth they had better be governed in the manner of the mainland and not according to the ethics of the Orient.

Ominously, he cautioned:

The dark-skinned citizens have been taught how far the American white man will go to protect his women from brutal assaults by men . . . Those in politics in Hawaii . . . must avoid stirring up ill feeling against the defense forces to gain political advantages . . . or else our National Congress may become convinced that, after all, self-government in Hawaii is a menace to the nation's naval security in the Pacific Ocean, and the sooner curtailed the better for the nation.

It was to remain the unalterable theme of his plaint until the day of his departure from the Islands.

Of her own departure from the Islands, Thalia Massie had ended her newspaper account with a simple expression of relief:

"At last we were on the road to a normal life once more. . . ."

It is hard to know what Thalia meant by a "normal life." Certainly her life up to that time seems to have been far from normal in the accepted sense of the word. It was true that her reactions had been "normal" enough to cause her to leap to her husband's defense because of the "vile and rotten" rumors which had so obsessed him that he eventually killed a man, willfully or not, in order to put a stop to them. Nonetheless, neither her reactions nor her behavior patterns appear to have been so normal in other respects.

In an attempt to discover how much truth there was in these rumors which Clarence Darrow, in his closing address to the jury, had emphatically declared he did not believe to be true, Pinkerton agents had made enquiries about Thalia's life in Hawaii.

From an informant who had once owned the home which Thalia and Tommy occupied, and who would go to the house occasionally to get his mail, they learned what they had already begun to suspect, that the Massies were not a happy couple.

The informant was asked to explain.

"One had only to be around them for a short time to notice it," he said. "Several times I have seen her put her arms around and kiss other men right in his presence, but he would say nothing. She was a heavy drinker, in fact both were, and I have seen her stewed many times."

Then he went on: "I had a friend who was in the Navy, and who lived not far from the Massies. This fellow told me he often called to see the Massies, and says he knows for a fact that when Mr. Massie would leave town for a few days as he very often did, that Mrs. Massie entertained men, all Navy officers, at her home, and he would see them come and go at all hours of the day and night."

While this account was suspiciously voyeuristic, hence dubious, the same could not be said of that furnished the Pinkerton men by Thalia's Japanese maid.

"During 1930 and 1931," she told them, when she was asked at what time a certain officer came to the house, "he came about once each week, but about May, 1931, he began to come oftener, and once stayed all week, while Mr. Massie was away. During this week, he slept in the Blue Room, and Mrs. Massie in her own room.

"They would go swimming at Waikiki, also went on picnics to Kailua, Nanakuli Beach, and sometimes would stay away two or three days, at which times she took sheets, pillow slips, towels and night clothes . . ."

Perfectly innocent though all this might have been, it was hardly the image of herself that Thalia had tried to convey to the jury when she was on the witness stand. Possibly it was closer to the image in the minds of those who knew her well, one of whom may very well have been the officer whose face she had slapped on that unguarded night at the Ala Wai Inn.

From a distinguished American, whose integrity both in naval and judicial circles is unquestioned, the Pinkerton agents learned that Thalia Massie was not thought of as an acceptable Navy wife. More explicitly, the agents were told that Thalia had the reputation of running around with various men, in fact associating with any man who looked prosperous and clean.

That this was disbelieved by Darrow or never fully disclosed to him, may be attributed to the fact that the Navy code would never have allowed it to be made public. The code would not permit a man like Tommy to openly doubt his wife's innocence. It would not permit a native to deny that he had raped her, in the face of her accusation that he had. Besides, had not she herself said: "Don't you know if there were any doubt I could never draw another easy breath?" To live by the code was to believe that a white woman, his wife, could not be mistaken.

Admirable though such loyalty to a code may have been in Navy circles, nevertheless, while the Rankin bill which would appoint a mainland governor over Hawaii was still being heatedly defended by Washington and just as heatedly opposed by the kamaiiana elite, while the Massie case itself was still being used as an argument to force Island submission to mainland authority, social circles in Washington and Honolulu were shocked to learn that Thalia was going to Reno to divorce her husband!

In announcing it to the press, she said that "the divorce is entirely Lieutenant Massie's desire. He feels the ties of marriage irksome and would rather be free."

Although she did not believe in divorce, she added, she would nevertheless give it to him. Did she love him so deeply that she would do anything he asked, a reporter wanted to know.

"Well—perhaps I'd better not say about that," she replied. "Let's just say I'm terribly fond of him and whatever he wants me to do, I will do gladly because he wants it."

The divorce, she insisted, had nothing to do with the Hawaii case. Yet it must surely have had something to do with the fact that the clamor for a mainland governor soon lost some of its motive power. The divorce had tarnished the ideal of American womanhood for which she had been the symbol. Her martyrdom could no longer be used as a weapon. The governorship of Hawaii finally went to

Joseph Boyd Poindexter, an Oregonian who had settled in Hawaii some years earlier to practice law.

It was the last starring role which Thalia was to play in the drama of Hawaii's racial conflict. A few months later, on a cruise to Europe, she slashed her wrists and flung herself screaming from the top deck of the liner, only to have her leap broken by a fall to a lower deck. The story of her attempted suicide was read with curiosity and pity. But it stirred no new anger against Hawaii. And, in Hawaii itself, changes had already begun to take place in the relationship between Haoles and non-Haoles. Whether it was because of the remarkable restraint which the non-Haole population had exercised throughout both trials, or because the Haoles themselves had finally discovered that the non-Haoles no longer were the imagined threat which seemed so menacing during the trials, it was becoming all too clear to the Haoles that white supremacy was incompatible with the composition of Hawaii's people.

And it was at this time, when the hue and cry for mainland domination of the Islands had lost much of its momentum, that Clarence Darrow wrote his final words on the Massie case and Hawaii:

Nature specially fitted this magic spot to help work out the old problems of race, with its loves, its hatreds, its hopes and fears. It seems fit that the Hawaiian Islands, basking in the great sea between the oldest and newest civilizations of the world, might one day lead the union of the diverse races of man. I would like to believe that this favored land might prove to be the place where the only claim to aristocracy would be the devotion to justice and truth and a real fellowship on earth.

Had he perhaps seen, in perspective now, that his anger at the verdict was mistaken—that his passion for justice and truth was not the white man's prerogative?

On July 2, 1963, a West Coast newspaper which, thirty years earlier, had for weeks devoted its front pages to the Massie case, reported that Thalia Massie had died in West Palm Beach, Florida, from an accidental overdose of barbiturates.

The story appeared on an inside page, together with a brief recapitulation of "the chain of events which rocked the Islands and the United States Navy."

What the story neglected to say, was that the Massie case was a decisive battle against white supremacy in Hawaii.

True, there is still no idealized union of the races in Hawaii such as Darrow foresaw. But neither has there been another Massie case. The roles which Thalia and Tommy Massie played in that case no longer have a racist audience to respond.

There are only the people of Hawaii—complex in their origins—sometimes unfair in their racial loyalties and prejudices—but vitally aware that an end to racial inequality is inevitable. This much the Massie case had taught them.

ABOUT THE AUTHORS

BOB THOMAS, the son of a newspaper editor and movie publicity executive, was born in San Diego, California in 1922. He joined Associated Press in 1943 and became a Hollywood columnist in 1944. In addition to writing numerous magazine articles, Bob Thomas has written *The Flesh Merchants*, *If I Knew Then* (with Debbie Reynolds), *The Art of Animation* (story of the Disney studios), *King Cohn* (biography of film tycoon Harry Cohn), *The One and Only Bing Crosby*, *Selznick*, *Thalberg*, and *Joan Crawford*. He is married and has three daughters.

PETER PACKER was born in London in 1916. At the age of eleven he won a Royal Society of Arts first prize in writing. He came to America in 1937 after one of his stories was accepted by *Esquire* magazine. He served in the U.S. Air Force, first as a buck private and then as a captain. His stories have been published in such magazines as *The New Yorker*, *Cosmopolitan*, *Liberty* and *American*. In between writing novels he has written documentary films and produced and written such television shows as Twentieth Century-Fox Hour, Kraft Theater, Ford Theater, My Friend Flicka, The Virginian, The Big Valley, Lost in Space and Death of the Other Self.

His novels include *White Crocus*, *Inward Voyage*, *The Love Thieves* and *A Summer Passion*. He is married and has two children.

The Days of Eternity

by
Gordon Glasco

Here is a breathtaking saga of a passionate love so overwhelming that it defies war, betrayal, conscience—and time itself. One Sunday morning, Anna Miceli, a successful American lawyer, sits in church and sees a man—and her heart stands still. At that moment, time melts away. Once again Anna is the innocent girl of an Italian country village. It is wartime, and the time of her first consuming love—for the young German lieutenant who commands the occupying forces. But when he commits an unspeakable act, Anna's world is shattered, her life changed forever. Now, twenty-eight years later, he stands before her—a priest. And now, Anna knows the time has come to face an agonizing choice. For here is the man whose memory has been a cold cinder of hatred inside her, the man she has vowed someday to destroy—and the man her turbulent heart can never surrender.

Read THE DAYS OF ETERNITY, on sale September 1, 1984, wherever Bantam paperbacks are sold, or use the handy coupon below for ordering: